Reversing Africa's Decline

Lester R. Brown
Edward C. Wolf

Worldwatch Paper 65
June 1985

HC
800
Z9
E536
1985

Financial support for this paper was provided by the United Nations Fund for Population Activities. Sections of the paper may be reproduced in magazines and newspapers with acknowledgment to Worldwatch Institute.

The views expressed are those of the authors and do not necessarily represent those of Worldwatch Institute and its directors, officers, or staff, or of the United Nations Fund for Population Activities.

Preface

This Worldwatch Paper focuses on a single continent, thus departing from earlier papers in a series that typically has dealt with global issues. We decided to focus on Africa because it is such a special situation, a continent experiencing a breakdown in the relationship between people and their natural support systems. Famine, and the threat of famine, are among the manifestations of this breakdown.

We have chosen to call this paper *Reversing Africa's Decline*. We believe the decline can be reversed; to do so will require an abrupt departure from the "business as usual" approach that African governments and the international community have mounted so far in response to the food crisis. Beneath the urgent work of providing food aid and resettling families displaced by famine, a long-term strategy of environmental restoration is essential to reversing recent trends. This paper highlights some of the themes that any successful strategy must embrace.

Most analyses of Africa's decline have focused on drought, the disarray of national economies, and the continent's tumultuous politics. Few have recognized that a new approach to development is required. The strategy we propose might be termed "resource-based." Slowing population growth, conserving soils, restoring forests and woodlands, and enhancing subsistence agriculture are sure to be cornerstones of successful efforts to reestablish working economies in Africa. These priorities can provide a foundation for African aspirations and an agenda for international assistance.

We are indebted to many people who shared with us their time, insight, and expertise. Edward Ayensu, Leonard Berry, Robert Browne, Michael Dow, Robert Goodland, Kenneth Hare, Linda Harrar, Norman Myers, Sharon Nicholson, Stephen Schneider, Jagadish Shukla, Jyoti Singh, Maurice Strong, J.A.N. Wallis, and Charles E. Weiss reviewed an early draft of the manuscript on short notice. Sharon Nicholson kindly permitted us to reproduce her unpublished data on rainfall in Africa. Hans Hurni in Ethiopia and Henry Elwell in Zimbabwe enriched our awareness of efforts in those countries to understand and confront land degradation. Angela Coyle provided invaluable research assistance. To all of them, we extend our appreciation; for errors that remain, we accept sole responsibility.

Lester R. Brown and Edward C. Wolf

Table of Contents

A report from the U.S. Embassy in Addis Ababa in 1978 indicated that the Ethiopian Highlands were losing over a billion tons of topsoil per year through erosion. Any agronomist who saw that report knew that unless immediate action was taken to arrest the loss, Ethiopia was headed for a famine even greater than the one that toppled Haile Selassie's government four years earlier. The only question was exactly when it would come.[1]

For those who are not agronomists, the reported loss of topsoil was an abstraction. Only when it translated into images of starving Ethiopian children on television screens around the world some six years later did this gradual loss of topsoil acquire a human dimension.

This Ethiopian example typifies what is happening in Africa today. Reports from agronomists, ecologists, foresters, hydrologists, and meteorologists indicate that growing human demands are eroding life support systems throughout the continent. The pieces of this emerging mosaic of a continent in decline are found in studies by United Nations agencies, the World Bank, the U.S. Agency for International Development, and others. As surely as soil erosion undermined agriculture in Ethiopia's Highlands, these trends of ecological deterioration, if not reversed, will undermine Africa's economic future.

Although essentially agrarian, Africa is losing the ability to feed itself. In 1984, 140 million of its 531 million people were fed entirely with grain from abroad. In 1985, the ranks of those fed from abroad, already nearly half as large as the population of North America, will almost certainly increase. A mid-February assessment of Africa's food situation by the United Nations reported that some 10 million people had left their villages in search of food, many of them crowded into hastily erected relief camps. In late April, the Economic Commission for Africa reported that starvation deaths had passed the one million mark, reminding people everywhere that space-age technologies and famine coexist.[2]

In Africa, as elsewhere in the Third World, cereals supply two-thirds to four-fifths of caloric intake, making per capita grain production a basic indicator of both economic productivity and individual welfare. During the two decades following World War II, grain production per person in Africa either remained steady or increased slightly, peaking in 1967 at 180 kilograms. This level, roughly one pound of grain per ·day, is widely viewed as the subsistence threshold, below which malnutrition begins to erode human development and labor productivity. Since 1967 per capita grain production has been declining. In 1983 and 1984, years in which low rainfall depressed the harvest, per capita grain production was 118 and 120 kilograms respectively, down more than a third from the peak. (See Figure 1.) Although the decline has been more precipitous in some countries than in others, few countries have escaped this trend.[3]

As per capita grain production has declined in this agrarian society, so has per capita income. The African ministers responsible for economic development and planning are now painfully aware of this trend. At an April 1985 meeting of the Economic Commission for Africa, they drafted a memorandum to the United Nations Economic and Social Council, which was in effect a plea for help. They observed that, "As a result of sluggish [economic] growth and a high rate of population growth, per capita income, which was growing at negligible rates during the seventies, has consistently declined since 1980 at an average annual rate of 4.1 per cent, and average per capita income is now between 15 and 25 per cent less than 15 years ago."[4]

In addition to declining per capita food production and income, Africa's foreign debt is growing, partly because of rising food imports. The region's cereal import bill climbed from $600 million in 1972 to $5.4 billion in 1983, a ninefold increase. By 1984 food imports claimed some 20 percent of total export earnings. Meanwhile, servicing the continent's debt, projected to reach $170 billion by the end of 1985, requires an additional 22 percent of export earnings.[5]

Kilograms
Per
Person

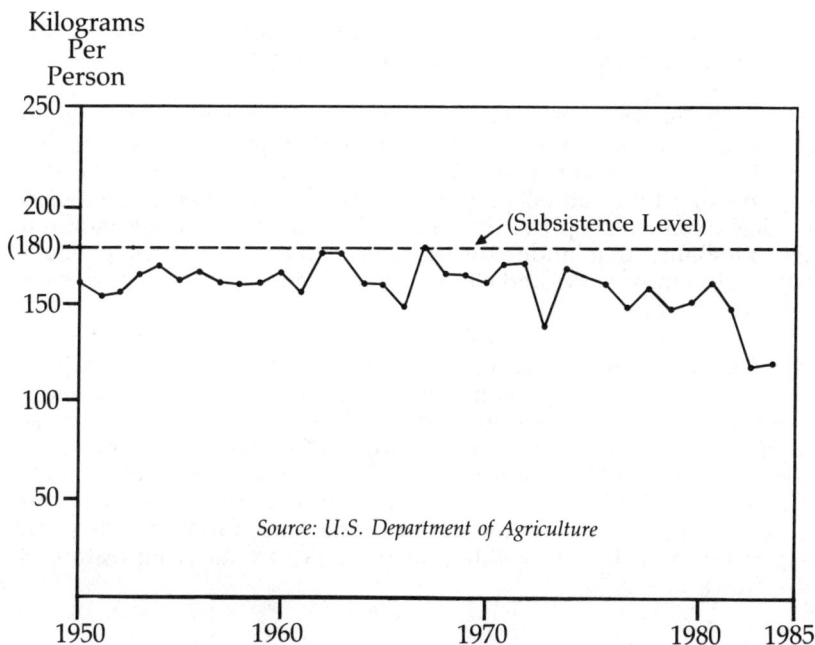

**Figure 1: Per Capita Grain Production
in Africa, 1950-84**

Africa's plight is rooted in its phenomenal rate of population growth—the fastest of any continent in history. The introduction of public health measures and vaccinations has reduced death rates, but without parallel efforts to reduce birth rates, overall population growth has accelerated. As a result, Africa's population is now expanding at 3 percent per year, or twentyfold per century.

This enormous growth in human numbers, now under way for a third of a century, is stressing natural support systems throughout the continent. In country after country, sustainable-yield thresholds of forests and grasslands are being breached. Soil erosion, the loss of soil organic matter, and the depletion of soil nutrients are diminishing land productivity over much of Africa.

10 Although the short-term effects of this environmental degradation are serious, accumulating evidence suggests that the continent-wide loss of vegetative cover and the degradation of soils may be disrupting long-term rainfall patterns as well. Though no meteorological models conclusively prove this link, policymakers must now confront the possibility that under the stresses imposed by growing populations, environmental and climatic deterioration are reinforcing each other in Africa.

At issue is whether national governments and international assistance agencies can fashion new, environmentally sound development strategies to reverse the ecological deterioration and economic decline that is inflicting such suffering on the people of Africa. The continuation of a "business as usual" policy toward Africa is to write off its future. Without a massive mobilization of resources, the prospect of reversing the decline in per capita grain production is poor, suggesting that famine will become chronic, an enduring feature of the African landscape.

Ecological Deterioration and Economic Decline

Assessing recent trends in Africa requires an understanding of changes in its ecology, climate, and economy. The key relationships are those between Africa's 551 million people and the natural resources and support systems—forests, grasslands, croplands, and water—that underpin its predominantly agrarian economy.

Evidence from soil scientists, agronomists, meteorologists, and economists indicates that sustained overuse of biological systems can set in motion changes that are self-reinforcing. Each stage of deterioration hastens the onset of the next. When destructive change is coupled with rapid population growth and subsistence economies, the stage for human tragedy is set.

How such complex, interrelated systems unravel has been described by World Bank energy analyst and ecologist Kenneth Newcombe. His model, based on fieldwork in Ethiopia, portrays a cascading decline in biological and economic productivity triggered by loss of tree cover. According to Newcombe, as people seek new agricultural land, natural forests retreat before the plow. Trees no longer recycle mineral nutrients from deep soil layers, and soil fertility begins to decline. In this first stage, wood supplies remain sufficient and the gradual erosion of cropland fertility is imperceptible.[6]

11

As rural and village populations grow, markets appear for wood, used both for construction and household fuels. Cutting wood from remnant forests generates income for peasant families, who now burn unmarketable crop residues and animal dung in their own households. Removing crop residues and diverting dung from fields degrades soil structure and leaves fields more vulnerable to erosion. The depletion of remaining forests accelerates, and the loss of soil fertility becomes noticeable.

Once nearby stands of trees are gone, dung and crop residues are traded in markets where formerly only wood was sold. The steady export of nutrients and organic matter from croplands severely limits crop yields and the ability of pastures to support livestock. Families depend more on the sale of dung and less on local harvests, for unreliable crop yields prove barely sufficient even for subsistence needs. On sloping fields, annual soil erosion of 50-100 tons per hectare is common.

Eventually, cow dung becomes the main fuel source in villages and thus the main cash crop from nearby farms. Rural families use crop residues for cooking and as forage for their livestock, which grazing land can no longer support. Pervasive topsoil depletion leaves farmers vulnerable to total crop failure during even routine dry seasons. In markets, both food and fuel prices rise rapidly.

At the final stage, biological productivity is destined to collapse. Families can no longer produce enough food for themselves or their livestock, let alone for markets. A massive exodus from rural areas begins, often triggered by drought that could formerly have been tolerated. Famine is widespread; peasants' lack of income is compounded by absolute shortages of food at any price.

This accelerating cycle of degradation is not theoretical. Newcombe observes that "this transition from the first to the final stage is in process right across Ethiopia and has reached the terminal phase in parts of Tigre and Eritrea."[7] At a World Bank workshop in Botswana in March 1985, Newcombe warned, "There is evidence that [the final stage] has already been reached in some areas of several countries in Southern Africa and that virtually every country has areas that have reached [the point at which wood gathering has overtaken land clearing as the major cause of deforestation]."[8]

The common theme in the cascading effect Newcombe describes is disruption of the self-regulating mechanisms of natural systems on which humans depend. Because the various stages of decline are predictable, the event that pushes the system into instability can be identified. Newcombe believes this "critical transition" occurs in subsistence economies when more trees are cut for fuel than to make way for farmland. Identifying countries that have passed this turning point is essential both to governments and to international assistance agencies.

The United Nations Food and Agriculture Organization (FAO) estimates that 60-70 percent of the outright clearing of forests and woodlands in tropical Africa is for agriculture. In many countries, however, wood collection for fuel and other uses exceeds the sustainable yield of remaining accessible forests. A 1980 World Bank survey of selected African countries showed that fuelwood demand exceeded estimated sustainable yields in 11 of 13 countries. Only in Senegal and Ghana could the annual growth of remaining woodlands still satisfy demand.[9]

The degree of imbalance varies widely among and within countries. In some, demand and sustainable yield of wood are severely out of balance; in others, only marginally so. For example, in both semi-arid Mauritania and mountainous Rwanda, firewood demand is ten times the sustainable yield of remaining forests. In Kenya, demand is five times the sustainable yield; in Ethiopia, Tanzania, and Nigeria, demand is 2.5 times the sustainable yield, and in Sudan, it is roughly double.[10]

13

Sudan's wood imbalance illustrates the interaction between rapidly expanding populations and their biological support systems. Estimates based on World Bank data indicate that national fuelwood consumption crossed the sustainable yield threshold somewhere around 1965. From then on, fuelwood consumption exceeded new tree growth, gradually diminishing both the forest stock each year's new growth. (See Figures 2 and 3.)

During the first years after the sustainable yield threshold was crossed, Sudan's forests changed little. After 20 years, forested area contracted by about one-fifth. In the next 20 years, however, expanding demand is likely to deplete all the remaining woodlands. During the first half of this 40-year-span, there is little indication of the problems coming in the second half. Once the mid-point is reached, only extraordinary efforts in family planning and tree planting can halt the system's complete collapse.

Closely paralleling the loss of tree cover in Africa is the deterioration of grasslands as livestock numbers expand nearly as fast as the human population. In 1950, Africa had 219 million people and a livestock population of 295 million. Since then, the continent's population has increased two and a half times, reaching 513 million in 1983. Livestock numbers have nearly doubled, increasing to 521 million in 1983.[11]

Because little grain is available for feeding livestock, the continent's 174 million cattle, 190 million sheep, and 157 million goats are supported almost entirely by grazing or browsing. Everywhere outside the tsetse fly belt, livestock are vital to the economy. But, in many countries, herds and flocks are diminishing the grass resource that sustains them.

An FAO report on the eight nations of southern Africa reveals the extent of overgrazing: "For some countries and major areas of others, present herds exceed the carrying capacity by 50 to 100 percent. This

Million
Cubic
Meters

150

Fuelwood
Consumption

100

50

New Tree Growth

Source: Derived from World Bank Data

1950   1960   1970   1980   1990   2000

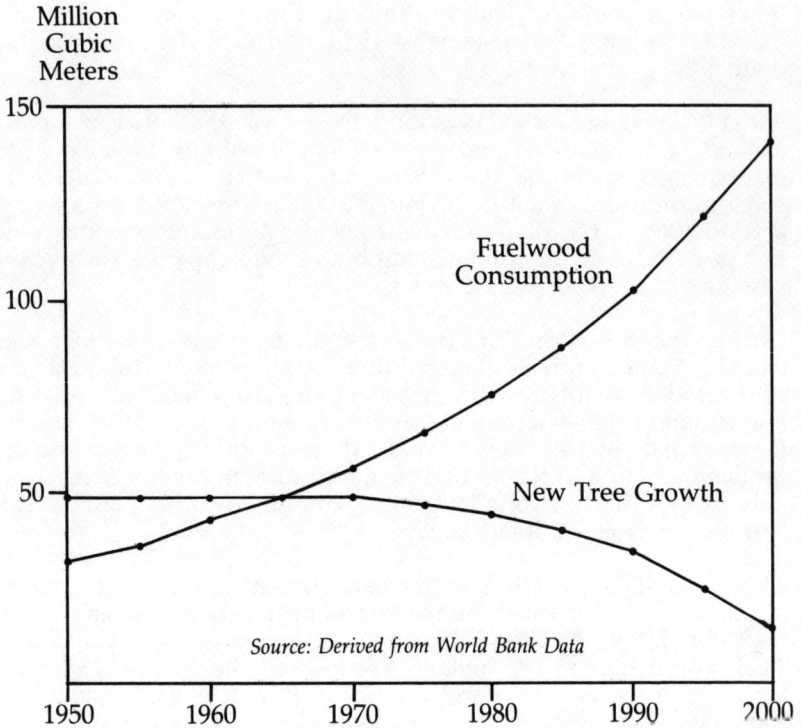

Figure 2: Fuelwood Consumption and New Tree Growth in the Sudan, 1950-80, With Projections to 2000

has led to deterioration of the soil—thereby lowering the carrying capacity even more—and to severe soil erosion in an accelerating cycle of degradation."[12] Heavy grazing, combined with declining rainfall, gradually changes the character of rangeland vegetation and its capacity to support livestock.

Million
Cubic
Meters

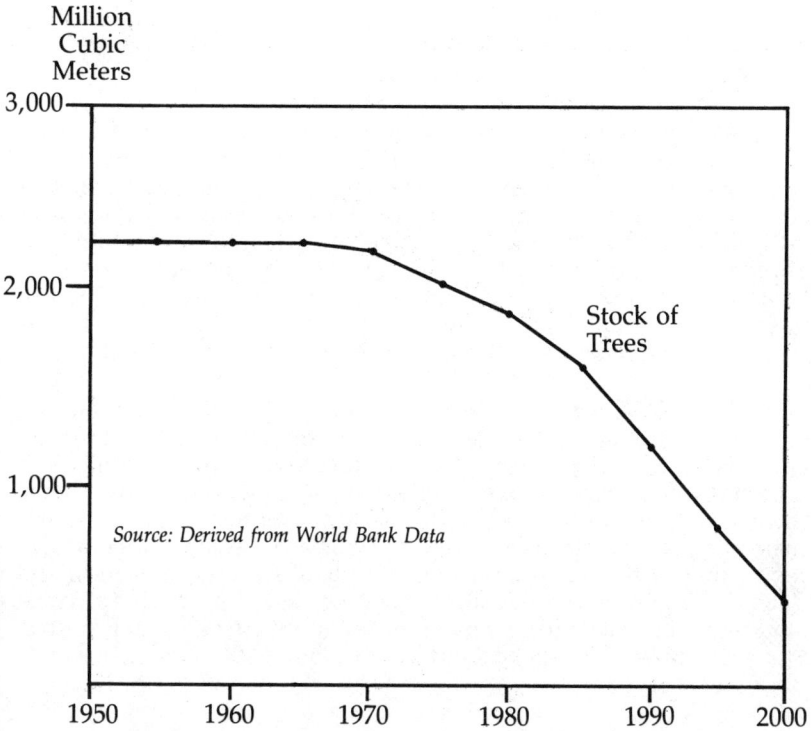

**Figure 3: Standing Stock of Trees in the Sudan, 1950-80,
With Projections to 2000**

As grazing and wood gathering increases in semi-arid regions,
rapidly-reproducing annual grasses replace perennial grasses and
woody perennial shrubs. The loss of trees like the acacias in the Sahel
(the band of semi-arid savanna that extends across Africa south of the
Sahara) means less forage in the dry season, when the protein-rich
pods of these trees feed livestock on otherwise barren rangeland.
Annual grasses that come to dominate the landscape are far more

sensitive to rainfall than perennials, and may not germinate at all in drought years. A range already shrinking as cultivated land expands cannot sustain smaller herds, even in wet years.

As Africa's grasslands have deteriorated, the composition of its livestock population has shifted. From 1950 to 1970, Africa's cattle population grew over 2 percent per year, somewhat faster than that of either sheep or goats. (See Table 1.) Since 1970, annual growth in cattle numbers has dropped to .83 percent, while the sheep and goat population has expanded an average of 2.27 percent. This shift toward sheep and goats that eat woody foliage reflects a period of unrelenting rainfall decline, loss of grass cover, and intensified pressure on the woodlands that supply fuel for human households.

The economic effects of progressive biological impoverishment are cumulative, direct, and sometimes catastrophic. Especially hurt are small farmers and the rural poor. Substituting crop residues and dung for wood fuels is one example of narrowing options. Another is the way farmers respond when declining soil fertility begins to reduce their harvests. World Bank analysts William Jones and Roberto Egli report that in the Great Lakes Highlands of Rwanda, Burundi, and Zaire, "As population densities have increased, particularly where land is most scarce, farmers have turned to tubers as a starch source. Statistics show a consistent and continuous displacement of grains

Table 1: Changes in Africa's Cattle, Sheep, and Goat Populations, 1950-70 and 1970-83

	Average Annual Change	
	1950-70	1970-83
	(percent)	(percent)
Cattle	+2.15	+0.83
Sheep	+1.67	+2.36
Goats	+1.67	+2.19

Source: Food and Agriculture Organization, *Production Yearbook* (Rome: various years).

and legumes by tubers, which yield more starch per hectare."[13] As farm sizes grow smaller and land productivity declines, farmers in some areas plant potatoes, cassava, or yams in place of corn to maximize the calories, rather than the protein, their fields produce. The loss of soil's nutrient and water-holding capacity at this subsistence level makes farmers even more vulnerable to drought.

The World Bank study provides a profile of the steady loss of options for rural livelihoods: "caloric value of diet per farm is maintained as farms grow smaller by substituting higher yielding tubers for higher food-quality grains; food crops for home consumption crowd out cash crops; livestock is reduced to small animals that live on crop and household waste; and emigration is needed to maintain a low-income equilibrium . . . . This pessimistic prognosis is a formula for survival— little more."[14]

No one questions that these forms of ecological and economic decline are under way in parts of Africa. Their pervasiveness, however, has not generally been noted. One attempt to assess the extent of degradation has been made by Leonard Berry of Clark University, who surveyed desertification trends in African countries for the United Nations Environment Programme. (See Table 2.)

These countries, representing a cross section of the continent, have a combined population of 281 million people, just over half Africa's total. The survey focused on five manifestations of desertification: sand dune encroachment, the deterioration of rangelands, forest depletion, the deterioration of irrigation systems, and problems in rainfed agriculture.

Not one of the 100 indicators—5 for each of the 20 countries—showed any improvement. For roughly one-fifth of the 100 indicators, the seven years under review saw no significant change. Almost half of the measurements showed a moderate deterioration. Over a quarter revealed serious deterioration. The three categories showing the most consistent deterioration were rangelands, forests, and rainfed agriculture.

Table 2: Desertification Trends in Selected African Countries, 1977-84

Country	Sand Dune Encroachment	Deterioration in Rangelands	Forest Depletion	Deterioration of Irrigation Systems	Rainfed Agriculture Problems
Botswana	+	+	o	o	o
Burkina Faso[1]	o	+	+	+	+ +
Cameroon	o	+	+	o	+
Chad	+ +	+ +	+	+ +	+ +
Ethiopia	+	+ +	+ +	+	+
Guinea	o	o	+	+	+ +
Kenya	o	+ +	+	o	+
Lesotho	na	+	+ +	o	+ +
Mali	+	+ +	+ +	+	+
Mauritania	+	+ +	+ +	+	+
Niger	+	+ +	+	+ +	+
Nigeria	o	+	+ +	o	+
Senegal	+	+ +	+	+	+ +
Somalia	+	+	+	+ +	+
Sudan	+ +	+	+	+	o
Swaziland	na	+	+ +	o	+ +
Tanzania	na	+	+	na	+ +
Uganda	o	+ +	o	o	+
Zambia	na	na	na	+	+
Zimbabwe	na	+ +	+	+	+ +

[1]Formerly Upper Volta.

Key: o = stable, + = some increase, + + = significant increase, na = not available or not applicable

Source: Adapted from Leonard Berry, "Desertification: Problems of Restoring Productivity In Dry Areas of Africa," presented to the 1985 Annual Meeting Symposium, African Development Bank, Brazzaville, People's Republic of the Congo, May 8, 1985.

The climatic, ecological, economic, and social trends reflected in the survey are clearly interdependent. All show signs of self-reinforcing deterioration that progressively robs the landscape of its resilience and reduces the economic choices open to people who depend on it.

Reduced rainfall has clearly intensified the continent's ecological deterioration. A troubling question is the extent to which environmental change has contributed to the rainfall decline. According to French meteorologist Robert Kandel, ". . . plant cover in general and forests in particular may have virtues going beyond the microclimate and extending to the regional-scale circulation." In a review of desertification in West Africa, World Bank forester Jean Gorse writes, ". . . the current 17-year dry period is most worrying. With population growing faster than ever before, the proposition that there is now a trend towards increasing aridity deserves a special research effort."[15]

Population-Induced Climate Change?

Since the late sixties much of Africa has suffered from below average rainfall. During the early seventies rainfall shortages were particularly acute in the Sahelian countries. During the early eighties drought has been more severe and widespread, affecting most of the continent. Rainfall levels in 1983 and 1984 in sub-Saharan Africa, where four-fifths of the continent's people live, were the lowest recorded during this century.[16]

Data gathered by meteorologist Sharon Nicholson from roughly 300 reporting sites record the extent of the decline in some 20 countries from 1901 to 1984. (See Figure 4.) Using an average of rainfall data for 1901 to 1974 as the norm, Nicholson calculated the annual percentage departures for the years 1901 to 1984. During the first six decades of the century, several clusters of drought years appear, the most severe of which ran from 1910 to 1914. Rainfall in 1913 was more than 40 percent below normal, a decline comparable to that of 1973, 1983, and 1984. The century's second decade saw eight consecutive years of below average rainfall. Other drought periods were typically less than half as long.[17]

Percent

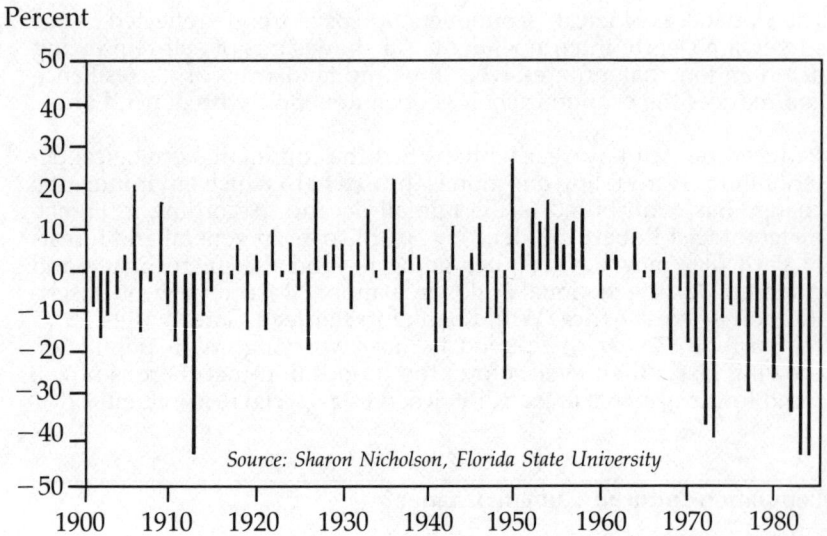

Source: Sharon Nicholson, Florida State University

**Figure 4: Rainfall Fluctuations in the Sahel and Sudan
Expressed as a Percent Departure from the Long-Term Mean,
1901-1984**

The 1910 to 1917 shortfall was matched by nine consecutive years of above average rainfall from 1950 to 1958. Since 1967, however, Africa has seen 17 straight years of below average rainfall. Of those 17 years, all but one have been at least 10 percent below the calculated norm, and the last two years have been more than 40 percent short.

Almost two decades of depressed rainfall raise a central question: is this a temporary decline or a new long-term trend? Decline may be due exclusively to oscillations in the global circulation of the sort that have caused droughts historically. Or it may be caused by vast land use changes such as deforestation that increase water runoff, reduce evapotranspiration, and increase reflectivity (albedo). If the dryness of the last 17 years is temporary, then governments should concentrate on emergency food relief while waiting for the rains to return. While greater investment in agriculture and family planning is unquestionably needed, much of the continent's food shortfall would be eliminated by the return of "normal" rainfall. If, however, population-induced changes in land use and soil degradation are gradually reducing average rainfall, then far more urgent and ambitious measures are needed.

Analyzing the current situation in Africa is complicated by a history of wide swings in rainfall that make it difficult to isolate human effects on climate. A climatic history of the Sahel over the last ten thousand years, for example, shows extreme fluctuations from periods of wetness to dryness. In just the last few centuries the Sahel has periodically experienced severe, prolonged drought. And early in this century, the particularly severe drought from 1910 to 1914 reduced the annual discharge of the Nile by 35 percent and the depth of Lake Chad by about half; river flows and lake levels fell throughout West Africa.[18]

Many meteorologists believe that the drought is a result of short term shifts in atmospheric circulation patterns. Meteorologist F. Kenneth Hare of the University of Toronto summarizes this view: "One school of thought—certainly dominant among professionals—says that the high incidence and prolonged duration of recent droughts are simply aspects of a natural fluctuation, due to some deep seated oscillation of the general circulation of the atmosphere (and maybe the ocean)."[19]

In an effort to understand how atmospheric circulation influences rainfall, some meteorologists have focused on changes in patterns of ocean surface temperature. Meteorologist Peter Lamb, for example, points out that drought in the Sahel is often associated with a southward shift of unusually warm water in the equatorial regions of the Atlantic just off West Africa. Dr. Eugene Rasmussen of the U.S. National Meteorological Center has investigated a correlation between the "El Niño/Southern Oscillation" phenomenon in the Pacific Ocean and sub-par rainfall in southeastern Africa. Rasmussen notes that rainfall in the region has dropped below normal during 22 of the last 28 El Niño episodes.[20]

Another source of reduced rainfall in Africa could be the changes in land use over vast stretches of the continent since mid-century. Almost all of these changes increase rainfall run-off, reduce evaporation from soil and transpiration from plants, and increase the reflectivity of the land. Meteorologists investigating the links between land use changes and climate are handicapped by poor land use data in most regions. No comprehensive effort has been made in Africa to measure changes in runoff, evapotranspiration, surface reflectivity, and other meteorological variables, or to analyze their combined effects on rainfall.

Any assessment of how land use changes affect rainfall must begin with our basic understanding of climatic systems. We know that rainfall over land comes from two sources—moisture-laden air masses moving inland from the oceans, and evapotranspiration over the land itself. The measured flow of all the world's rivers amounts to one-third of the total rainfall over land. Assuming no long-term change in the amount of water in the oceans, this runoff, via rivers, would be balanced by the airborne moisture moving inland from the oceans. This would leave the remaining two-thirds of the rainfall over the continents to be accounted for by evapotranspiration. If changes in runoff and evapotranspiration are large enough, they might reduce rainfall over parts of Africa.

Virtually all of the land use changes associated with population growth in Africa decrease vegetative cover. This change increases the share of rainfall that returns to the ocean via streams and rivers and reduces the amount of rainfall retained, eventually to be evaporated. A particularly strong complementary relationship exists between trees and clouds. Trees collect underground water and convert it into vapor through transpiration; clouds condense water vapor into liquid in the form of rainfall. If trees are removed this cycle is weakened.[21]

The seasonal rains of tropical Africa (rains on which virtually all of the northern half of the continent depends) follow the movement of a zone at which northeasterly trade winds and southwesterly trade winds meet, called the "intertropical convergence zone" (ITCZ). The convergence zone follows the latitude of greatest solar intensity, moving north during the Northern Hemisphere summer, reaching as

"If changes in runoff and
evapotranspiration are large enough,
they might reduce rainfall over parts
of Africa."

far as the northern limit of the Sahel. Air bearing moisture evaporated over the Gulf of Guinea is drawn toward the low pressure zone of the ITCZ and becomes rainfall when atmospheric turbulence lifts it rapidly enough for the water vapor to cool and condense. Whether rain falls depends partly on the quantity of moisture in the air, including that from the ocean and from evaporation over land; where it falls depends on factors that cause moist air to rise.[22]

The forests of the West African coast from Senegal to the Zaire basin may be a key to whether sufficient moisture reaches the continent's interior during the summer monsoon. Evidence from meteorological models and from observations in the Amazon Basin suggests that some of the moisture carried long distances over the continents is "recycled" by forests along the way—falling as rain and then returned to the air by evapotranspiration. Some of the moisture runs off and returns to the ocean in rivers. When forests are cleared, runoff increases and evapotranspiration is reduced.[23] The disappearance of intact forests in West African coastal countries such as the Ivory Coast and Nigeria may be diminishing water recycling and reducing the amount of water vapor available to generate rainfall once it reaches the turbulent convergence zone over the Sahel during the rainy season.

Whether the moisture-laden air that reaches the band of savannas across sub-Saharan Africa is forced to rise and condense depends partly on local conditions that generate upward convection, particularly vegetation. The Sahara itself tends to remain cloudless and rainless (and, therefore, bare) partly because its surface is more reflective than vegetated land. This region emits more heat than it receives from the sun; the source of heat that equalizes this apparent imbalance is an atmospheric process called "subsidence," the sinking of hot, dry air. This dry, high pressure air suppresses cloud formation and rainfall in desert latitudes.[24]

Meteorologist J. G. Charney and his colleagues proposed a mechanism by which desert conditions might spread beyond their normal boundaries. Clearing woodlands and degrading grasslands by overgrazing increases the land's albedo. The decline of absorbed sunlight, combined with the reduced evapotranspiration expected when vegetation is disturbed, counteracts cloud formation and rainfall. The diminished rainfall, in turn, dries out the landscape and further reinforces desertification.[25]

Although this "biometeorological feedback" has not been confirmed to be the cause of drought in Africa, theoretical models of the dynamics of the atmosphere have tended to validate Charney's hypothesis as a mechanism for perpetuating the drought. The persistence of drought in the southern, generally wetter parts of the Sahel may be due in part to this kind of self-reinforcing action. The biometeorological feedback hypothesis is further supported by modelling studies by Jagadish Shukla and Yale Mintz of the University of Maryland, who showed that reduction in evaporation over land can also reduce rainfall over land.[26]

Data on land use changes have not been systematically gathered for most African countries, but enough data exist to give some sense of the broad shifts occurring. These changes take several forms, including deforestation, grassland deterioration, cropland expansion, desert expansion, forest degradation, and soil degradation.

The destruction of tree cover in Africa represents one of the most dramatic human alterations of the environment on record. Nearly every country in Africa is affected. In two countries, Mauritania and Rwanda, forests have virtually disappeared. The climatically critical rainforests of West Africa are disappearing at the rate of 5 percent annually. The Ivory Coast, which once had 30 million hectares of tropical rainforests, now has only 4.5 million hectares. Vast areas of Ethiopia, the communal lands of Zimbabwe, and the homelands of South Africa are now largely devoid of trees.[27]

As the forests shrink, cropland expands. Between 1950 and 1985 the area planted in cereals alone expanded from 46 million hectares to over 70 million. The area in all crops now approaches 120 million hectares. Much of the newly plowed land is steeply sloping, and runoff is proportionately greater.[28]

"Vast areas of Ethiopia, the
communal lands of Zimbabwe, and
the homelands of South Africa are
now largely devoid of trees."

Africa's deserts are expanding. An action plan for the Sahel prepared by the United Nations Sudano-Sahelian Office observes that "In 1983 alone the desert (Sahara) advanced at least 150 kilometers to the south."[29] Desert-like conditions are also being created throughout Africa by land mismanagement.

25

Meteorologists generally contend that deforestation or land use changes must affect an area of 25 million hectares (the area of a region 500 kilometers on a side) before climatic effects appear. Few seem aware that far more extensive changes have occurred, and are continuing, over the period during which rainfall has declined. Since mid-century, for example, nearly 25 million hectares of land have been brought under grain cultivation. The Ivory Coast alone has seen as much land deforested. Though annual changes seem less cause for alarm, their aggregate consequences can no longer be dismissed.[30]

Along with the outright loss of forests, remaining woodlands are being degraded both by firewood gathering and by shorter fallow cycles of shifting cultivators. With shifting cultivation, for each hectare of land actually growing crops, several hectares are in some stage of fallow, awaiting the return of fertility that will again sustain harvests. The United Nations Food and Agriculture Organization estimates that 178 million hectares of African forests and woodland are in such fallow. Under mounting population pressure, farmers cut fallow cycles too short to restore fertility, thus slowly degrading the vegetation.[31]

Soils too are being degraded all across Africa. Erosion is a major source of degradation, but the widespread use of cow dung and crop residues for fuel means that the organic matter in soils is declining and that soil structure is deteriorating. One consequence of the degradation of the remaining forests, grasslands, and soils is an increase in runoff and a reduction in soil moisture that, in turn, reduces evapotranspiration.

Scientists studying the hydrology of the Amazon Basin have acknowledged the importance of the scale of land use changes in influencing that region's climate. "Hydrologists have been inclined to discount the possibility that changes in land use can affect rainfall," wrote Brazilian scientists Eneas Salati and Peter Vose in an article in *Science* magazine. "This may be true if the area being converted is small in relation to the whole geographical-climatological zone and if the major proportion of the precipitation is advective and not dependent on recycling. However, it is almost certainly a fallacy where large amounts of water are being lost to the system through the greatly increased runoff associated with widespread deforestation and where the existing rainfall regime is greatly dependent on recycling."[32]

The conversion of tropical forests to cropland dramatically alters the hydrological cycle. Little research has been done on this in Africa. But research on a watershed in the central Amazon indicates that when rain falls on a healthy stand of tropical rain forest, roughly one-fourth runs off, returning to the ocean, while three-fourths re-enters the atmosphere either as direct evaporation, or indirectly through the transpiration of plants. After the rain forest is cleared for cropping or logging this ratio is roughly reversed, with three-fourths of the rainfall running off immediately and one-fourth evaporating to recharge rainclouds.[33]

A project undertaken recently at Zimbabwe's Hatcliffe Research Station shows how land use changes affect rainfall runoff. Using plots of land with a 4.5 percent slope, agronomist Henry Elwell of Zimbabwe's Ministry of Agriculture measured runoff under varying land use conditions, ranging from undisturbed natural vegetation to bare soil. (See Table 3.) In a typical year he found that only 1 percent of the rain falling on natural vegetation ran off. For clipped grass, used to approximate runoff from grasslands with controlled grazing, Elwell found that 8 percent of the annual rainfall ran off. On land planted in soybeans the figure increased to 20 percent, with much of the runoff occurring early in the rainy season while the soybean plants were small. On the plot that was left bare, 35 percent of the rainfall was lost.

The extent of runoff varies from site to site, depending on soil type and the intensity of rainfall. In much of Zimbabwe, for example, annual rainfall approaches that of Western Europe. But while rain in Europe falls throughout the year, Zimbabwe's is concentrated in a

Table 3: Rainfall Runoff Under Varying Land Uses At Hatcliffe Research Station, Zimbabwe (4.5 percent slope)

Vegetative Cover	Share of Annual Rainfall Running Off
	(percent)
Natural Vegetation[1]	1
Clipped grass	8
Soybeans	20
Bare soil	35

[1]Mostly tall grass, ungrazed.

Source: Personal communication with H.A. Elwell, Institute of Agricultural Engineering, Ministry of Agriculture, Harare, Zimbabwe, May 2, 1985.

three or four month season, suggesting a much greater potential for runoff and erosion. Slope is also an all-important variable affecting runoff. The 4.5 percent slope used at Hatcliffe is gentle compared with much of the land under the plow in Africa today. As the slope increases, so does the runoff and the likely erosion.

The effect of such land use changes increases in importance with distance from the coast, as the recharge of clouds by evaporation becomes the dominant source of rainfall in the interior. Any land use changes that reduce the recycling of water inland are also likely to reduce rainfall. Even in semi-arid regions, evaporation supplies much of the moisture and rainfall. In the Sahel, half to two-thirds of the region's rainfall may be derived from soil moisture.[34]

Given the lack of meteorological models detailing the relationship between changes in land use and possible changes in rainfall, any assessment at this point necessarily rests on a much simpler analysis. That vegetation declines increase runoff and reduce evaporation cannot be seriously questioned. What is lacking is an understanding of exactly how a decline in evaporation affects rainfall. Both the timing and persistence of low rainfall years suggest trends that one might expect if population-induced land use changes were affecting rainfall. In 1950 Africa's population was 219 million; as recently as 1960 it was 285 million; in 1985 it is 551 million. Initially, the annual additions were scarcely 5 million, but during the eighties they have averaged nearly 15 million. Given the cumulative effect of this accelerating population growth on land use and soil degradation, the effect on rainfall would be expected to appear during the latter part of the 1950-84 period, as is indeed the case. This is also consistent with the mechanisms postulated in the modelling studies of Charney, and Shukla and Mintz, which would work simultaneously and additively to reduce rainfall over Africa.[35]

Additional data consistent with the thesis that land use changes are reducing rainfall are the trends in increased desertification. Although desertification can be caused by either human mismanagement or below normal rainfall, the geographic pervasiveness of the African trends is consistent with the notion that land use changes are reducing rainfall.

The environmental changes that may be reducing rainfall are the same as those that make systems more vulnerable to drought. Deforestation, grassland deterioration, soil erosion, and soil degradation all increase vulnerability to drought. As the layer of topsoil dwindles and as organic matter content falls, the soil assimilates and stores less moisture. Under these conditions, land productivity would decline even if rainfall were normal.

As the evidence accumulates, it raises questions as to whether the term "drought" is appropriate to describe recent below normal rainfall. Drought implies that things will shortly return to normal, which may be misleading. It might be more accurate to refer to the dryness as a "reduction in rainfall," leaving open the question of whether this is simply a consequence of oscillations in the general atmospheric circulation, or whether it is also being influenced by devegetation and soil degradation. If rainfall in Africa is being reduced by changes in land use associated with population growth, the label "drought" is a disservice to policymakers, and certainly to the people affected.

"The environmental changes that may be reducing rainfall are the same as those that make systems more vulnerable to drought."

It is time to take seriously the idea that ecological deterioration and rainfall declines may be reinforcing each other, leading to a drier climatic regime over vast areas. Recent pressures on land are far more extensive than commonly believed; the capacity of a deteriorating ecosystem to sustain an African population expected to double by the first decade of the next century is in doubt.

29

Meteorologists traditionally have paid little attention to the effects of changing land uses on climate, but a growing minority is beginning to acknowledge this possible connection. Representative of this group is Canadian meteorologist F. Kenneth Hare, who concluded in an analysis of desertification in Africa, "we seem to have arrived at a critical moment in the history of mankind's relation to climate. For the first time we may be on the threshold of man-induced climate change."[36]

While scientists have years of work ahead in investigating the dynamics of Africa's climate, policymakers cannot wait for scientific certainty. They must respond instead to the evaluation of available evidence and anticipate the most likely outcome of a given situation. At issue is whether the rainfall decline over much of Africa in recent years is temporary—a drought that will end shortly—or whether it is an early stage of a long-term decline, one associated with the changes in land use and soil degradation that are disrupting the hydrological cycle. If it is the latter then rainfall will continue to decline as long as these changes continue.

Policymakers who confront the possibility of a deteriorating climate face at the same time the reality that per capita grain production is steadily declining in Africa, that national economies are disintegrating, and that international assistance to Africa is declining in real terms while the continent's population continues to expand at 3 percent each year. Any effort to reverse these interwoven trends must be undertaken quickly. The longer the delay and the further the relationship between people and natural support systems unravels, the more difficult it will become to reverse Africa's decline.

Braking Population Growth

Perhaps no other continent's destiny has been so shaped by population growth as has Africa's in the late twentieth century. Not only is its population growth the fastest of any continent in history, but in country after country, demands of escalating human numbers are exceeding the sustainable yield of local life support systems—croplands, grasslands, and forests. Each year Africa's farmers attempt to feed 16 million additional people, roughly 10 times the annual addition of North America or Europe.[37]

According to United Nations projections, Africa's 1980 population of just under 500 million will triple within a 45-year-span, reaching 1.5 billion by 2025.[38] Virtually all African governments will have to contend with the population growth momentum built-in when populations are dominated by young people born since 1970. In some African societies children under age 15 constitute almost half the total population, a share far higher than in most countries. (See Table 4.) This enormous group of young people will reach reproductive age by the end of the century.

At the continental level, population projections seem abstract, but they become more meaningful when individual countries are examined. In Ethiopia, whose starving people have come to exemplify the current crisis, fertility is not expected to decline to replacement level until 2045. Given the country's age structure, World Bank demographers project that the number of Ethiopians will rise until it reaches 231 million, six times the current population. In a country whose soils are so eroded that many farmers can no longer feed themselves, this growth appears unrealistic, to say the least.[39]

Nigeria, the most populous country in Africa with 91 million people, suffers a similiar plight. If it attains replacement level fertility in 2035, its population will eventually reach 618 million, more people than now live in all of Africa. Nigeria is particularly vulnerable because its enormous surge in population is being supported by imported grain, financed almost entirely by oil exports. But, by the end of the century, Nigeria's oil reserves will be largely depleted.[40]

Table 4: Share of Population Under Age Fifteen in Selected Countries, 1984

Country	Share
	(percent)
Kenya	50
Nigeria	48
Zimbabwe	48
Algeria	47
Ghana	47
Bangladesh	46
Morocco	46
Tanzania	46
Zaire	45
Mexico	44
Ethiopia	43
South Africa	42
Egypt	39
India	39
Brazil	37
China	34
Soviet Union	25
Japan	23
United States	22
West Germany	18

Source: Population Reference Bureau, *1984 World Population Data Sheet* (Washington, D.C.: 1984)

These projections for two of Africa's most populous countries illustrate some of the difficulties ahead. But narrow demographics do not fully reveal the deterioration of basic life support systems that is under way in so much of the continent. In one African country after another, pressure on those systems is excessive, as shown by dwindling forests, eroding soils, and falling water tables. If African governments take a serious look at future population/resource balances, as China did almost a decade ago, they may discover that they are forced to choose between a sharp reduction in birth rates or falling living standards and, in some cases, rising death rates.

If African governments choose to do nothing, the "demographic transition" that has marked the advance of all developed countries may be reversed for the first time in modern history. All African countries have now moved beyond the first stage of this transition, with its equilibrium between high birth and death rates. But virtually all remain stuck in the second stage, with high birth rates and low death rates. In this stage, population growth typically peaks at 3 percent or so per year.

If living standards were to continue to rise, African countries would be following the normal path toward the third and final stage of the demographic transition. Their populations would eventually again be in equilibrium, with low birth rates and low death rates, as they now are in much of Western Europe. Unfortunately, many African countries are no longer progressing toward the third stage. Those that do not will eventually return to the equilibrium of the first—high birth and high death rates. Nature provides no long-term alternative. But getting the brakes on population growth by reducing birth rates will be extraordinarily difficult for all African governments, especially in those countries where the average couple now has five to eight children. Yet, the alternative may be an Ethiopian-type situation where population growth is checked by famine.

Public attitudes will not change without strong political leadership. Until recently, Africa's leaders have regarded population growth as an asset, not a threat. In their view Africa was too sparsely populated. Unfortunately, they failed to recognize that Africa's soils are often thin and not particularly fertile, and that much of the continent is arid or semi-arid. In addition, Africa's leaders have been slow to grasp the arithmetic of their population growth. Many saw the difference between a 1 percent and 3 percent annual growth rate as relatively innocuous. But a population growing 1 percent annually will not even triple in a century, while one growing 3 percent annually will increase some twentyfold.

"After a long silence on the
population issue, key African leaders
are now making it a matter of public
discussion."

Belatedly, some African leaders are beginning to sense the desperation inherent in existing population trends. A 1983 assessment of Africa's future by the Economic Commission for Africa reported that "the historical trend scenario is almost a nightmare . . . The potential population explosion would have tremendous repercussions on the region's physical resources such as land . . . At the national level, the socio-economic conditions would be characterized by the degradation of the very essence of human dignity. The rural population . . . will face an almost disastrous situation of land scarcity whereby whole families would have to subsist on a mere hectare of land." A World Bank analysis of Africa's economic outlook described the Commission's assessment as "graphic but realistic."[41]

33

One sign of new concern over population growth is a surge in requests to both the United Nations Fund for Population Activities and the World Bank for family planning assistance from African governments over the last 18-24 months. Although these requests will take time to translate into smaller families, they are a step in the right direction.

As recently as 1974, when the United Nations Conference on Population was held in Bucharest, only two countries in sub-Saharan Africa—Kenya and Ghana—had policies to reduce population growth. By mid-1984, 13 countries had such policies. The additional countries included: Botswana, Burundi, Gambia, Lesotho, Nigeria, Rwanda, Senegal, Uganda, Zambia, South Africa and Zimbabwe. U.S. demographer Thomas Goliber points out that of this group, five had explicit fertility reduction goals. Botswana wanted to increase contraceptive use to 15 percent of all couples of reproductive age by 1985; Ghana planned to reduce population growth to 2 percent annually by the year 2000; Kenya to 3.3 percent by 1988; Rwanda to 3.5 percent by 1986; and Uganda to 2.6 percent by 1995.[42]

At an early 1984 conference on population convened by the Economic Commission for Africa in Arusha, Tanzania, the 36 assembled countries observed that, "Current high levels of fertility and mortality give rise to great concern about the region's ability to maintain even [those] living standards already attained since independence." Conference attendees adopted the Kilimanjaro Program of Action on Population, which called on Commission-member states to "Ensure the availability and accessibility of family planning services to all couples or individuals seeking such services freely or at subsidized prices."[43]

Some national political leaders have spoken out strongly on population in recent years. Among the most vocal has been Kenya's President Daniel Arap Moi, whose public addresses regularly refer to the need to reduce population growth. More recently, Nigeria's head of state, Major General Muhammadu Buhari, has issued statements in support of family planning. Buhari's support was conveyed by the Nigerian delegation to the UN Conference on Population held in Mexico City in August, 1984. It reported that, "The Government now recognizes, more than ever before, the fact that the overall rate of growth has to be brought down to the level at which it will not impose excessive burdens on the economy in the long run. The Government plans to achieve this through an integrated approach to population planning."[44] After a long silence on the population issue, key African leaders are now making it a matter of public discussion.

Among the African countries with family planning programs, Zimbabwe's may be the most vigorous. In early 1985 demand for family planning services outstripped projections, forcing the government to request an emergency air shipment of contraceptives from the United States. In a continent where emergency food shipments dominate the news, such a request is a welcome development. According to a recent survey, some 21 percent of married women of reproductive age in Zimbabwe are practicing contraception. More important, this figure is growing rapidly.[45]

Discussions with Zimbabwean officials and farmers suggest at least three reasons for the soaring interest in limiting family size. First, since local communities are responsible for educational services beyond primary school, they finance secondary school education largely by assessing student educational fees. For parents who want a good education for their children, the incentive to reduce family size is strong. Second is increased awareness in rural areas, where most Zimbabweans live, that growth in family size will no longer be matched by growth in cropland area. Third, contraceptive services are readily available through community-based distribution centers now operating throughout Zimbabwe. People can now consciously weigh the advantages of planning their families, whereas in the past, they could not. In effect, the supply of family planning services is generating its own demand.

Any assessment of the effort required to stabilize population must recognize two gaps in family planning. One is the unmet demand for family planning services that already exists. This gap can be filled by increased investment and a locally based distribution system for both technical advice and contraceptives. The second gap is the difference between family size desired by individual couples and that required eventually to halt population growth.

The first gap is quite large in some developing countries, particularly those in Central America, Brazil, and the Andean countries. Africa, however, has a rather small unmet need for family planning. In a survey of ten African countries, the share of women who said that they wanted no more children ranged from 4 to 17 percent. The typical African woman would like to have several children, with the desired number as high as nine in Mauritania.[46]

The magnitude of the effort needed to halt population growth in Africa is outlined in recent studies by the Population Institute and the World Bank. The Population Institute used the announced population goals of four countries in Africa in its assessment. Egypt, for example, wants to reduce its population growth rate from 2.7 percent at present to roughly 1 percent by the year 2000. The other three countries have established somewhat similar fertility reduction goals.[47]

The cost of providing family planning services to achieve these goals, though substantial, is modest indeed compared with the ecological, economic, and social costs of inaction. The Population Institute notes that funds would come from four sources—individual couples who pay some or all of the expense of the contraceptives they use, private family planning organizations, governments of the countries in question, and international family planning groups.

36

The World Bank estimates that adoption of a "rapid" fertility decline goal in sub-Saharan Africa would require a twentyfold increase in expenditures by the end of this century. Meeting such a goal, which would require a 16 percent annual growth in family planning expenditures, would be more than offset by reduced public expenditures in other sectors. Savings in education expenditures alone in the year 2000 would reach $6 or more per capita in a country such as Zimbabwe.[48]

These projected expenditures over the next 15 years are not beyond reach. Yet, they cover only the first gap in family planning—the provision of services. For the typical African country, bridging the second gap—that between desired family size and the much smaller family required to meet stated national population goals—will mean reducing average family size from today's five or six children to about two by the year 2000. This may not be possible without substantial financial incentives or disincentives, such as those now being used in China to encourage one-child families. Wherever desired family size exceeds that which is consistent with the goals for social improvement, substantial expenditures or penalties may be required to reconcile the two.

Successful family planning programs vary widely, but all have common characteristics. In many developing countries, a head of state who both understands the arithmetic of population growth and is committed to taking action has made family planning markedly easier. Enthusiastic and visible support is crucial.

Closely related to this commitment at the top is the setting of goals and the allocation of responsibility for achieving them. Regular monitoring is also essential. During the late seventies, for example, President Suharto of Indonesia instituted quarterly meetings with the provincial governors to review the family planning programs. These discussions permitted a timely sharing of information that helped overcome obstacles at the local level. And the meetings themselves demonstrated Suharto's personal concern with population growth.

Some countries have effectively used support by well-known athletes and film stars to promote family planning, and others, such as Mexico, have worked family planning themes into popular soap operas. Such efforts establish quick social acceptance of family planning and national population policies.

Experience has repeatedly shown that grassroots programs—those staffed and led by local people—work best. Their advice is always more acceptable than that of an outsider brought in specifically to promote a program. Convenience and cost are also important. Surveys show that couples wishing to control their fertility are unlikely to travel more than an hour to reach a family planning service center. If services are too costly, they go unused. One reason for the surge in demand for contraception in Zimbabwe, noted earlier, was the decision to provide services without cost to those with annual incomes below $150 per year.

Family planning programs that work best offer a full range of contraceptives and sterilization for both males and females. The more kinds of contraceptives offered, the more likely couples will find a method that meets their particular needs. For personal or medical reasons, some contraceptives may not be acceptable. When couples are satisfied with a contraceptive method, continued use is far more likely.

Given the unprecedented numbers of young people who will reach reproductive age in Africa within the next two decades, the adoption of a two-child family as a social goal may be the key to restoring a sustained improvement in living standards. Success in striving for two children per couple will bring problems of its own, including a severe distortion of age group distribution. But it may be the price many societies will have to pay for neglecting population policy for too long.

Restoring African Soils

Africa's croplands are not among the world's oldest, but few regions have a poorer natural endowment of productive soils. Glaciers that left fertile mineral paths across Europe and North America never reached Africa. Nutrient-poor soils over much of the continent face months of intense sunshine followed by punishing seasonal rains that can carry away exposed topsoil in sheets.

38 On this vulnerable land base, Africa's total harvests of cereal grains have doubled since mid-century. But while the yields of wheat, maize, and rice have risen modestly, the yields of subsistence staples, including sorghum and millet, have been stagnant or even declining. Food production on the continent has increased primarily by expanding the cultivated area—often onto steep land with unstable soils, or into forests whose thin soils are quickly depleted by a few seasons of plowing. In the Sahel, millet and sorghum harvests have increased even more slowly than the outright increase in cultivated area, indicating that agriculture has advanced onto marginal land that cannot sustain yields. The need to keep this land in production in good years and bad has hastened erosion.[49]

Since 1920, over 90 million hectares of land have been opened to cultivation in Africa—the largest increase for any continent. During the sixties, cultivated area in Africa grew three times faster than in Asia, even while the "Green Revolution," which bypassed Africa, was encouraging double-cropping and making cropland expansion lucrative in Asia. In the seventies, the rate fell off. By the mid-seventies, the only land still available to agriculture in many African countries was generally unsuited to sustained farming. Throughout the continent, inherent fertility was being depleted by erosion and exhaustion.[50]

Despite its pervasiveness, the erosion of Africa's soils is not easy to assess. Reliable data on which to base continental or even regional estimates are scarce. Satellite images of vegetation tell something about crop yields, and aerial photographs of dust plumes off deserts reveal serious wind erosion, but such large-scale assessments mean little at the local level. None of Africa's major rivers carries a silt load as great as that carried by the rivers of Asia and Latin America; sediment doesn't sound the alarm in Africa that it does in the Ganges of India or China's Huang He (Yellow River). But this measure of soil erosion can seriously understate the severity of erosion farmers experience. In Ethiopia's Wollo province, for example, sediment measured in a stream draining a heavily-farmed watershed indicated soil loss of less than two tons per hectare each year. But individual fields within the same watershed experienced annual soil losses as high as 80 tons per hectare.[51]

Much soil ends up in the bottomlands along river courses, where it might seem that the accumulated nutrients would make for fertile farmland. But, according to the Ethiopian Highlands Reclamation Study, sponsored by the government's Ministry of Agriculture and the UN Food and Agriculture Organization, these deposited soils are too heavy for traditional plows. They also remain waterlogged during the growing season—their infertility the result of the loss of organic material and water-holding capacity from the steep fields above.[52]

This tragic irony highlights the nature of Africa's soil problems. Steep fields are cleared of plant cover and then cultivated. Slash-and-burn cultivators clear regenerating forests after just a few years of fallow. Wherever agriculture has pushed beyond the limits of truly arable land, soil erosion is likely to be excessive. In the watershed in Wollo Province described above, nearly half of all the land is plowed. The other half is used to graze oxen. In Rwanda, annual and perennial crops now occupy more than 90 percent of all the potential agricultural land each year. In such areas, where land is no longer left in trees to maintain the watershed, or where hillsides are plowed, crop yields have begun to decline.[53]

Even where harvests seem to belie erosion problems, soil loss can be serious. Zimbabwe has achieved a remarkable recovery from drought, with a 1985 harvest estimated to be double the country's requirements. Yet the country's Natural Resources Board estimates that half the communal land farmed by peasants is already severely eroded. By early in the next century, lands now considered good may be unable to produce even subsistence yields.[54]

The steady deterioration that limits farmers' economic options as it robs their soils of nutrients leaves them virtually certain victims of drought. Measures of rainfall captured in weather-station gauges tell little of the water actually available to crops when soils are eroded and unable to absorb and store water. This is especially true in the semi-arid tropics where rain comes only in a few months of the year; in sub-Saharan Africa, moisture retained in the root zone of the soil must provide the "rainfall" of the many months that skies remain cloudless.

In its 1981 report, *Accelerated Development in Sub-Saharan Africa*, the World Bank announced that "A strategy to stop the accelerating degradation of soils and vegetation is overdue."[55] After four more years of agricultural decline, the strategy remains overdue. Restoring the ·fertility of African soils, restraining agriculture on unsuitable land, and making it far more productive on the best land deserve priority attention from African governments and the international community.

Part of the reason for past neglect of conservation has been the lack of immediate, tangible benefits from erosion control. As another World Bank report points out, "Soil conservation is a peculiar category because it is not an end in itself; you cannot eat it or sell it; as an intermediate product, it is useful only to the extent that it results in some future flow of agricultural production that would not have existed without it."[56] In regions where harvests have failed, however, farm families have a direct interest in soil conservation projects.

In areas such as Ethiopia's Highlands, where pressures on soils are severe and drought has left vast areas barren, physical protection of the landscape will have to accompany the country's efforts to resettle families and reintroduce cultivation. Building and maintaining terraces and drainage ditches on sloping land will be essential in some areas to preserve remnants of natural fertility for years of better rainfall.

Ethiopia illustrates both the potential and the pitfalls of large-scale efforts to conserve soils. In 1977, the new government launched a massive program in several provinces to construct soil conserving terraces and drains. The campaign mobilized subsistence farmers through the country's Peasant Associations and marshalled international assistance from the United Nations and World Food Programme for "food for work" and "cash for work" programs. By 1984, 590,000 kilometers of contour ditches called "bunds" had been con-

"In sub-Saharan Africa, moisture
retained in the root zone of the soil
must provide the 'rainfall' of the
many months that skies remain
cloudless."

structed and trees had been planted on 150,000 hectares of erosion-prone slopes. Yet of 500 million tree seedlings distributed from nurseries for planting, only 15 percent survived—reflecting drought, careless planting to fill quotas, and poor choice of tree species.[57]

41

One promising step taken in Ethiopia was the creation in 1981 of an applied research program to assess the country's conservation efforts, recommend techniques, and monitor erosion in several agricultural areas. With staff from the University of Berne, Switzerland, and support from the United Nations University, the Soil Conservation Research Project has trained Ethiopian technicians and gathered four years of information on erosion rates and conservation work. As soil conservation programs begin in other African countries, similar sustained research will be essential to evaluate progress and refine techniques.[58]

Kenya, with a long history of soil conservation efforts, offers an example of a promising combination of conservation and new farming practices that increases the land's vegetative cover and reduces the likelihood of severe erosion. In 1974, the Kenyan Ministry of Agriculture began a soil conservation extension program with the assistance of the Swedish International Development Authority. Farmers were encouraged to terrace sloping land by leaving unplowed strips along the contour. To compensate farmers for the economic penalty of leaving some land out of crop production, the government distributed fruit and fuelwood tree seedlings and cuttings of quality fodder grasses for the unplowed strips. Tree crops diversified the produce farmers could sell. High-quality fodder enabled farmers to restrain the destructive free grazing of cattle. Terraces retained water and soil nutrients and visibly raised yields on their upslope side. In the semi-arid Machakos district, maize production in some fields actually increased by half after introduction of the terraces.[59]

In contrast with Ethiopia, the Kenyan program takes a market-oriented approach, letting farmers choose which practices to adopt and which trees to plant. By 1983, terraces had been built on 100,000 farms, and extension agents were reaching over 30,000 new farms each year. To succeed in the long-run, however, farmers must perform the necessary time-consuming maintenance in the years ahead, and practices must continue as landholdings change hands. Though the country's agricultural land is far from stabilized, the "Kenyan model" can be adopted in other African countries.[60]

Despite their agronomic advantages, terraces have drawbacks. On steep slopes where constructing terraces requires excavation, the labor involved can be prohibitive. Where farmers have reached the limits of the available arable land, as they have in the Ethiopian Highlands and in some central African areas, leaving terraces in grass rather than crops reduces the cropped area, adding to short-term food aid needs. And terraces must be maintained and, in some cases, rebuilt every year, as experience in Ethiopia has shown. In Rwanda and Burundi, contour ditches introduced by colonial governments to control soil loss have been abandoned since independence because farmers feel the ditches are not worth the maintenance they require.[61]

While terraces are needed in some places to slow soil loss, particularly where land is likely to remain in continuous production, soil scientist Michael Stocking of the University of East Anglia argues that "the only *real* way of controlling erosion rates is through vegetative protection, whether directly through high-input farming and dense stands of monocrops or indirectly through fertility-enhancing farming systems aimed at the small farmer."[62] Developing and introducing such fertility-enhancing systems has become a major goal of agricultural research in Africa. One of the more promising approaches in humid areas is to grow crops without plowing at all.

Since 1974, Rattan Lal and his colleagues at the International Institute of Tropical Agriculture (IITA) in Ibadan, Nigeria, have been studying low-cost minimum tillage and no-till systems for humid and sub-humid areas in Africa. No-till methods, which involve planting directly into a stubble mulch and using herbicides for weed control, can reduce soil losses to nearly zero, increase the capacity of cropland to absorb and store water, and reduce the energy and labor needed to produce a harvest. Perhaps most important, Lal points out that "no-tillage generally out-yields the conventional tillage systems if the crops suffer from moisture, temperature, or nutritional stress."[63]

An IITA report sketches the rationale for farming systems that reduce or eliminate plowing: "Erosion must be prevented by keeping a continuous ground cover, and by avoiding soil compaction from the use of machinery. Organic matter must be maintained by the use of mulch. And leaching must be countered, as it is in the natural forest and in the long-fallow system of shifting cultivation, by deep-rooted trees or plants, which pump nutrients up into the foliage, from which they ultimately fall back into the soil."[64]

Minimum tillage systems that maintain the productivity of cropland offer an alternative to shifting cultivation and a chance to remove some marginal land from cultivation entirely. Where unplowed land is still available and, therefore, shifting cultivation is unlikely to be abandoned, the fertility of fallow land can sometimes be restored quickly. A research project in Nyabusindu, Rwanda, has developed an "intensive fallow" using deep-rooted legumes when land is taken out of production; World Bank analysts report that "the soil fertility improvement achieved within one year with this type of fallow is remarkable."[65] Where new land remains available for clearing, however, or where livestock are allowed to graze fallow land, farmers may be slow to change their fallow practices.

On fertile land, as much biological activity occurs in the topsoil itself as in the crops it sustains. The renewed interest in intercropping, minimum tillage, and managed fallows has rekindled investigation of the soil organisms that synthesize and release plant nutrients in the absence of artificial fertilizer. Little is known about the ecology of microbes in the soil. Since fertilizer-intensive farming certainly will not reach most African farmers in the near future, research on biological fertility, especially nitrogen fixation, can complement soil conservation efforts. In early 1984, the International Union of Biological Sciences proposed a major collaborative research program to "determine the management options for improving tropical soil fertility through biological processes."[66]

While slowing severe erosion and improving low-input shifting cultivation practices are important, the momentum of population growth in African countries demands more radical changes in African agriculture. According to Ermond Hartmans, Director of the IITA, "in the long run Africa's growing population can be fed only if traditional systems are changed . . . The solution of Africa's food crisis will not be by a gradual evolution of existing systems only."[67] The revolution in farming systems that conserves soil and permits continuous cultivation will take African agriculture back to its cultural and climatic roots—a savanna agriculture patterned on the natural vegetation that it replaces.

On savannas, trees and grasses grow together. There is no closed forest or unbroken prairie. A number of new agricultural methods, known collectively as agroforestry, mimic this natural relationship by combining useful tree crops with cultivated food crops. Agroforestry systems can be tailored to the desiccated Sahel and to the moist farmlands of equatorial and coastal West Africa. Their universal appeal is reduced soil erosion, increased nutrient cycling and biological activity in the topsoil, and resistance to drought. The trees used in agroforestry can help secure physical terraces on sloping land, reinforcing physical soil-conserving structures. The World Bank's study of Rwanda, Burundi, and Zaire points out that "the existing hundreds of thousands of square kilometers of terraced land should be considered as a huge sunken capital left over from colonial times . . . The stabilization of these terraces would be a first step for future introduction of agro-forestry farming systems and changes in land use."[68]

For humid areas, the IITA and the Nairobi-based International Council for Research in Agroforestry are investigating an agroforestry technique called alley cropping. Rows of crop plants are grown between hedgerows of trees or perennial shrubs. Prunings from the trees mulch the crops, returning nutrients to the soil. Fast-growing, nitrogen-fixing trees like leucaena work well in this system, improving the soil and providing the farmer with fuelwood and fodder. Alley cropping recovers soil fertility in the same way that traditional bush-fallow methods do, but permits continuous cultivation.[69]

In parts of the semi-arid Sahel, traditional agroforestry methods based on the native acacia trees have been abandoned, and seasonal grazing lands have been converted to cropland. Many valuable trees

"Alley cropping recovers soil fertility in the same way that traditional bush-fallow methods do, but permits continuous cultivation."

and perennial grasses have disappeared from the landscape. Research in Senegal reveals some of the advantages of reintroducing native nitrogen-fixing trees to agriculture in the Sahel: "Yields of millet and groundnuts grown under *Acacia albida* trees on infertile soils increase from 500 kilograms per hectare to 900 kilograms per hectare. In addition to increased crop yields, there are 50-100 percent increases in soil organic matter, improved soil structure, increased water-holding capacity, and a marked increase in soil microbiological activity beneath the trees."[70] As with alley cropping in wetter lands, agroforestry in the Sahelian countries can shorten fallow intervals and reduce the pressure to expand farming onto marginal land.

45

Agroforestry and tree planting can help control another major cause of soil deterioration in Africa—overgrazing. Tree crops like leucaena and the acacias offer higher-quality forage than the grasses that grow beneath them; where farmers use foliage for stall feeding, they reduce the impact of livestock on their cropland. The apple-ring acacia (*Acacia albida*) of West Africa bears its foliage and pods in the dry season, offering protein-rich feed when grasses are in short supply. Shelterbelts planted on grazing land to reduce wind erosion act as living fences. Used to divide common pastures into private corrals, shelterbelts can give settled farmers who raise livestock the incentive they need to improve pastures. This approach, however, is inappropriate for nomadic herdsmen.

Restoring the productivity of African soils will require a different approach than the Green Revolution in Asia. The restoration of land productivity in Africa depends on restraining cultivation on marginal and steep lands and on making the most suitable land more productive. In contrast to Asia, where the overriding goal was to combine abundant water and artificial fertilizers to raise crop yields, the immediate target in Africa must be to restore vegetation and soils to make the most of limited water supplies. Africa's own green transformation will depend on breaking the cycle of land degradation. If soils are secured and vegetation is restored, crop yields will begin to rise toward their potential.

Replanting African Forests

The future of Africa's forests lies in farmers' hands. Most African farmers can increase harvests to feed growing populations only by clearing new fields, often at the expense of forests. Rising urban demand for fuelwood, which offers a steady source of cash to rural families, increases the demands on woodlands. As trees disappear, landscapes steadily become less fit for agriculture. The new forests on which Africa's future depends will have to help make farming more secure and productive.

Agriculture's imprint on African woodlands is clear from an FAO survey of the forest resources of 37 African countries. Forest land in fallow (recovering its woody vegetation after several seasons of cultivation) covers 178 million hectares, one-fourth as much land as the continent's remaining 685 million hectares of intact forests. Another 443 million hectares are shrub land; the spread of extensive farming is adding to this category, since shortened fallow intervals prevent the regrowth of anything but shrubs on what was previously well-wooded land.[71]

Overall, about 3.6 million hectares of African forests are cleared each year, an annual rate of about half of 1 percent of remaining forests. Shifting cultivation accounts for 70 percent of the clearing of closed-canopy forests and 60 percent of the cutting of savanna forests, according to the FAO. In parts of the continent, however, permanent forest clearing is accelerating.

The continent-wide rates understate the regional pressures on forest resources. The moist forests of coastal West Africa (the countries from Guinea through eastern Nigeria) were being cleared by commercial loggers and subsistence farmers by more than 5 percent each year in the early eighties. At this rate, these forests have a "half-life" of just 13 years. Well over half of all the outright deforestation in Africa takes place in these coastal states, which contain only 7 percent of the continent's forests. (See Table 5.) Though small by comparison with the vast remaining forests of the Zaire Basin, this coastal greenbelt of rainforests may play a critical role in recycling moisture from the Gulf of Guinea that provides summer rains from Senegal to the Sudan.

Table 5: Africa: Clearing of Closed Forests by Major Forested Region, 1985

Region	Area of Closed Forest	Annual Clearing	Change
	(thousand hectares)		(percent)
Coastal West Africa	13,752	703	5.1
Zaire Basin	171,540	351	0.2
East Africa	12,957	105	0.8
Total	198,249	1,159	0.6

Source: Worldwatch Institute estimates based on Food and Agriculture Organization, *Tropical Forest Resources*, Forestry Paper 30 (Rome: 1982).

While clearing land for farming has caused the largest absolute changes in Africa's forested area, mushrooming demand for household fuels and the growth of urban markets for fuelwood and charcoal relentlessly degrade remaining African woodlands. Firewood is Africa's primary fuel, and supplying it is the continent's largest industry. In most African countries, households use ten times as much wood as all other commercial fuels combined. Even oil-exporting Nigeria uses twice as much firewood as all other energy sources. According to Dennis Anderson and Robert Fishwick, authors of a World Bank study on fuelwood consumption and deforestation in Africa, "about 90 percent or more of the population are dependent on fuelwood, animal dung, or crop residues for heating and cooking."[72]

The effects of forest decline are most directly felt in the countryside, for trees provide the framework of economic life for rural Africans. Trees supply foods, medicines, fuelwood, and building materials, as well as fodder for livestock. Rural people rarely chop down standing trees for fuel. They may do so if the wood can be sold, but most of the fuel for rural households is gathered. Dead wood, shrubs, crop residues, and dung can be readily collected. Branches of living trees may sometimes be lopped off for fuel, or trees harvested to supply building poles, but usually these trees have a chance to regenerate. When wood harvests from living trees exceed what is grown in a year, trees eventually die. As woodland quality declines, rural communities get less wood, fodder, wildlife, medicines, fruits, nuts, and foliage each year.

Despite a decade of rapidly increasing international support for reforestation, little progress has been made toward restoring African woodlands and managing forests. After sustained drought led to famine during the early seventies, a partnership of European countries and Sahelian nations created the Club du Sahel to promote drought recovery and long-term development. Forestry and ecological restoration were high on the Club du Sahel's agenda. Starting from a base of only $2.9 million in 1975, international assistance to forestry and reforestation in the Sahel grew more rapidly than any other development sector, reaching $45.3 million in 1980. Over that period, nearly $105 million was spent to restore forests and supply wood for fuel and building in the region. Yet this rapid growth represented just 1.4 percent of the total international assistance to the Sahel in those years.[73]

Much the same pattern was repeated throughout Africa by major international donors. The U.S. Agency for International Development budgeted nearly $220 million to forestry and fuelwood projects in Africa between 1977 and 1984, although the annual amount committed has declined since 1982. The World Bank had spent nearly $93 million on fuelwood projects alone before 1983, and between 1968 and 1984, the Bank invested $426 million in African forest management, watershed protection, or agricultural development with a forestry component.[74]

Despite all the spending on trees, World Bank forestry advisor John Spears wrote in 1984: "The challenge remains of how to multiply what are in many cases relatively small scale initiatives, particularly in countries like Rwanda and Burundi, into larger scale rural forestry programs that will penetrate throughout the rural areas as quickly as possible. The current rate of tree planting in many Bank member countries is less than one-fifth (in many small African countries one-twentieth) of the rate needed to assure a reasonable supply of fuelwood, fodder, and poles by the year 2000."[75]

A comparison of rates of tree planting with rates of deforestation supports this conclusion. FAO's survey of African forest resources showed that the area of forests cleared each year exceeds the area on which trees are deliberately planted by a ratio of 29 to 1, far higher than any other region in the developing world. If degradation and unsustainable harvest of woodlands is added, the ratio would be higher still.[76]

Most of the international agencies that support forestry have begun a thorough reexamination of their reforestation efforts. New recognition of the complex relationship between forests, farmland, and household fuel supplies is beginning to influence the way money is spent to plant trees. The traditional rationale for forestry programs—that impending wood shortages simply mean the more trees planted, the better—is no longer a reasonable guide to setting planting priorities. Without question, more trees must be planted in Africa. But which trees, in which regions, for whom and by whom are the critical questions that will determine whether the next decade of replanting in Africa fares better than the last.

Around Africa's expanding cities the conventional wisdom may still apply. Plantations of fast-growing trees that can supply fuelwood and charcoal to city dwellers are essential. Plantations now supply less than 5 percent of Africa's fuelwood demands, and perhaps less than one-sixth of the wood and charcoal burned in cities and towns. Opportunities for plantations near settlements are far from exhausted, and the technical experience to establish and manage plantations can be put to best use near cities where a commercial market can justify the steep investment—up to $1,000 per hectare—they require.[77]

In much of the Sahel, however, plantations to supply cities are impractical. Even in wet years, water supplies are simply too meager to support the fast-growing tree species on which most plantation schemes have been based. Research to identify and develop prolific varieties of drought-tolerant native trees should be supported and expanded. But natural woodlands must be managed better as well, and wood supplies must be used more efficiently. Policies to slow population growth can help restrain unmanageable future demands.

Plantations anywhere must be seen as long-term propositions. The World Bank has outlined a long-term planting strategy to fill the urban wood fuel needs in Ethiopia by establishing nearly a million hectares of plantations near cities by the turn of the century, reaching an annual level of planting of 80,000 hectares by 1996. Even this ambitious planting program, which would cost several hundred million dollars, would not close the gap between supply and demand for wood fuel for 30 years.[78]

Plantations near cities and towns can begin to offset some of the steady drain of trees and dung from rural areas. The loss of organic matter and the cycle of land degradation that reduces farm productivity is well advanced in many parts of Africa. Farm families that cut wood to sell along roads to the traders who transport it into cities are not compensated for the steady deterioration of their environment. As U.S. AID forestry advisor Thomas Catterson points out, "The fact is that in many areas, not just in Africa, both the forests and the peasants are being exploited to provide cheap energy to the urban areas."[79]

The income that rural families receive from selling gathered wood or dung in towns is small but significant. In parts of Ethiopia, sales of dung to town markets may account for as much as 30 percent of family cash income. As plantations cut into these earnings, policies to make agriculture and small rural industries more profitable can help offset the lost income. Support prices for crops can make agriculture a more reliable livelihood. In Ethiopia, the dung diverted from farmland could add an estimated 1-1.5 million tons of grain to the country's harvests. Supplying the lost nutrients with imported commercial fertilizers would cost $123 million. Yet many farmers can now sell the dung for more than the additional grain.[80]

In rural areas, where most African families still live, trees should be planted not primarily for fuelwood but to restore fertility and productivity to agricultural land. Though household cooking fuels are no less vital for rural families than for city dwellers, dispersed and self-reliant rural families provide no market for plantations, even if plantations could be planted on the necessary scale. By emphasizing the role trees play in soil fertility and stable farming systems, reforestation efforts can enlist the help of rural families. Professional foresters working year-round cannot possibly oversee the necessary planting effort. By contrast, Anderson and Fishwick of the World Bank estimate that if tree seedlings can be provided to families to plant and maintain on their own lands, even assuming that they devote no more than ten days each year to caring for them, the workforce would be 40-400 times larger than even the largest national forestry service.[81]

51

Reintroducing agroforestry in its various forms could rebuild African traditions in which crops, livestock, and trees are integrated as a matter of course. Most research on agroforestry has emphasized reintroducing trees on cultivated land and grazing land. Researchers at the International Council for Research in Agroforestry argue that farmers and foresters might both benefit from agroforestry in remaining intact forests. National forest reserves in many countries simply cannot be adequately protected from agricultural settlement. Encouraging the interplanting of trees and crops where forest boundaries have been breached will establish some common interest between farmers and foresters and expand the potential labor force for forest management.[82]

Careful management of Africa's forests can boost wood supplies more cheaply than any alternative planting scheme. Africa still has over a billion hectares of forests and shrub land from which firewood, building materials, medicines, and wild foods are gathered. U.S. AID forester Thomas Catterson points out that "even modest gains in productivity could have significant impact on the fuelwood supply."[83] The cost of restoring degraded but intact forests to productivity could be as low as $200 per hectare—one-fifth the cost of many intensive plantations. Natural forests maintain hydrologic and nutrient cycles and are an important refuge for wild plant and animal species—critical functions often excluded from cost-benefit calculations. Natural forests also provide the best environment for the germination of tree seedlings, and can be an important source of trees for propagation in reforestation programs.

Where drought has killed trees, standing deadwood provides a fuel source that can be systematically exploited before living woodlands are cleared. In Senegal, drought-killed forests north of Dakar are now licensed to charcoal producers who supply much of the charcoal used in the capital. Surviving trees in drought-afflicted areas can also be surveyed to find hardy seedstock for reforestation efforts.[84]

In areas with no local tradition of agroforestry, rural families often grow trees for fruit, building poles, or shade around dwellings. In one Tanzanian village, residents claimed to have planted between 100 and 1,000 trees apiece. In Fatick, Senegal, families plant a variety of trees on their land and many maintain family tree nurseries. Encouraging and providing seedlings for such spontaneous planting can restore trees to the landscape far more cheaply and effectively than large-scale plantations.[85]

Any tree planting in the extensive crescent of savannas from the western Sahel to South Africa will have to consider the impact of livestock. The sale of livestock due to drought, and the migration of pastoralists from grazing lands that can no longer sustain their herds, has tragically disrupted a traditional way of life. But adjustments now may offer opportunities to restore productivity to some of Africa's rangelands. Livestock can be managed to favor the regeneration of woodlands. Controlled grazing allows trees to better compete with grasses for soil moisture. Young seedlings, however, require several seasons of protection from grazing, so rangeland reforestation requires cooperation from pastoralists if it is to succeed.

Reforestation and agroforestry depend as much on managing wood demand as on expanding supplies. In the next few years, before plantations can produce enough wood to offset forest losses in many countries, boosting wood-use efficiency in cities is particularly important. Many countries have short-term alternative fuels in the form of logging wastes and wastes from large state and commercial farms. In Ethiopia, the waste from forests cleared each year to establish state farms in the southern provinces could reportedly supply the entire annual charcoal demand of Addis Ababa. The crop residues of state farms and coffee plantations, sawmill wastes, and charcoal burned inefficiently could match the annual energy yield of an estimated 163,000 hectares of intensive plantations. The World Bank reports that these waste-based fuels could quickly contribute to the urban market with an investment of roughly $55 million, about one-third the cost of developing plantations to supply the same amount of fuel.[86]

53

Sophisticated tools can sometimes help transform fundamental problems, and scaled-up reforestation programs can take advantage of proven biotechnologies to screen useful tree species and propagate large numbers for planting. Poor genetic quality accounts for part of the failure of past planting efforts. According to international forestry consultant Fred Weber, "in the average nursery, we are still raising genetic garbage."[87] Better screening and selection of trees that survive droughts and perform well in marginal environments is likely to increase success rates markedly.

Once superior trees are identified, cuttings and tissue cultures can propagate them cheaply in large numbers. Though few African laboratories carry out this kind of work, they are not costly to establish; Ghanaian biologist Edward Ayensu of the Smithsonian Institution and the United Nations University estimates that a modest tissue culture laboratory capable of propagating useful trees for a national forestry program need cost no more than $160,000. Such facilities may be a key to providing high quality seedlings in large numbers to the African countryside.[88]

As important as the trees themselves are the symbiotic fungi and microorganisms that play a critical role in supplying nutrients and water in harsh environments. Since commercial fertilizers will not likely be used on a large scale in African reforestation efforts, research on nitrogen-fixing microbes and fungi that improve the uptake of phosphorus (especially short in many African soils) deserves high priority. Simple techniques for inoculating tree seedlings with the proper bacteria and fungi can dramatically increase plantation survival rates and boost the productivity of trees planted. Research on nitrogen-fixing bacteria and acacia trees is under way at the West African Microbiological Resources Center in Senegal. Involving institutes and universities from other parts of Africa could expand the use of symbiotic microbes in tree-planting programs and help reduce costly losses.[89]

Selecting suitable trees and designing technologies to quickly propagate and establish them will be useless unless trees are made available to the farm families who must plant and maintain them. Michael Dow of the the U.S. National Academy of Sciences speaks of a "genetic supermarket" offering an array of tree seeds and seedlings that would allow farmers to choose familiar species and those that fit their specific economic and environmental needs.[90] Anderson and Fishwick of the World Bank argue for a decentralized network of tree nurseries as the key to successful rural tree planting programs, concluding that "ideally, there should be a small tree nursery at every market center in Africa."[91]

Scaled-up planting and forest management must include women as foresters and organizers. Though women and children gather most of the wood and forest products, Africa has few women foresters, and women's attitudes on forest resource problems are rarely investigated. Wangari Maathai, the charismatic founder of Kenya's Green Belt movement (a grassroots effort to supply seedlings and help to people who want to start tree nurseries) exemplifies the leadership that women can provide to reforestation throughout Africa. The Women's Auxiliary in Dakar, Senegal, plans to start a similar tree growing effort in West Africa.[92]

Restoring African woodlands and forests is essential to the recovery of agriculture on which the continent's economic prospects depend. It will require sustained effort and cooperation among African governments and an unprecedented willingness by international donors to acknowledge the needs and defer to the judgment of the rural people who will do the bulk of the planting, maintenance, and forest management. These 380 million men, women, and children in the African countryside comprise the only labor force large enough to turn Africa's forest decline around. No simpler rationale for restoring woodlands throughout Africa is needed than an observation by West African foresters recalled by U.S. consultant Fred Weber: "regardless of how well all other rural development efforts may succeed, a Sahel without trees is dead."[93]

> "Though women and children gather
> most of the wood and forest products,
> Africa has few women foresters."

Getting Agriculture Moving

By almost any standard, agriculture is not doing well in Africa. Declining per capita food output, falling land productivity, rising food imports, and famine are among the most visible failures. This vast, largely agrarian continent is losing the capacity to feed itself, in part because of record population growth and the associated deterioration of the agricultural resource base. Agriculture also suffers from low priority and prestige, national food price policies that discourage investment, and declining rainfall. Per capita grain production in Africa has fallen by roughly one-third since 1970. But more serious, there is nothing in prospect on either the agricultural or the family planning side of the food-population equation to reverse this trend.

Within Africa, agriculture suffers from neglect in all but a few countries. International aid programs have focused on specific projects rather than overriding issues such as food pricing policy. Too often this assistance has been directed at the symptoms of Africa's agricultural stresses rather than the causes. Fortunately, awareness of these shortcomings is slowly spreading. World Bank Senior Vice President Ernest Stern describes the situation as follows, "We, along with other donors, I think it is fair to say, among all our achievements, have failed in Africa. We have not fully understood the problems, we have not identified the priorities, we have not always designed our projects to fit both the agroclimatic conditions of Africa and the social, cultural, and political frameworks of Africa . . . we, and everybody else, are still unclear about what can be done in agriculture in Africa."[94]

A 1981 report from the International Institute of Tropical Agriculture (IITA) summarized the African dilemma, "In Africa, almost every problem is more acute than elsewhere. Topsoils are more fragile, and more subject to erosion and degradation. Irrigation covers a smaller fraction of the cultivated area . . . leaving agriculture exposed to the vicissitudes of an irregular rainfall pattern. The infrastructure, both physical and institutional, is weaker. The shortage of trained people is more serious. The flight from the land is more precipitate . . . In one respect, namely the failure to develop farming systems capable of high and sustained rates of production growth, the problems of Africa have reached the stage of crisis."[95]

As Africa's population approaches 600 million, agricultural systems of shifting cultivation that evolved over centuries, and that were ecologically stable as recently as mid-century when population was only 219 million, are breaking down. Under the pressure of population growth, marginal land is being plowed and fallow cycles are being shortened. The same IITA report observes, "The African farmer has given many proofs of his ingenuity, but has found no way of overcoming the progressive decline in yields that results when fallow periods are reduced below a critical level."[96] The new agricultural technologies and inputs needed to offset such productivity losses either have not been developed or are not being applied.

One reason for Africa's agricultural disappointment is the expectation that dramatic advances in grain production that began in Asia some two decades ago could be repeated. Unfortunately, differences between the two continents make it impossible to transfer the Asian formula to Africa. For example, Asian agriculture is dominated by wet rice cultivation. A single package of successful yield-raising rice technologies could be easily adapted for use throughout the region. Indeed, essentially the same approach was used for Asia's second food staple, wheat, most of which is also irrigated. Africa, by contrast, depends on several food staples—corn, wheat, sorghum, millet, barley and rice among the cereals, plus cassava and yams—and a highly heterogenous collection of resilient farming systems.

Even more important, much of Africa is semi-arid, which limits the profitable use of yield-raising inputs such as fertilizer. The more dramatic gains in food production have occurred in Asia and elsewhere, where abundant moisture enables crops to respond strongly to chemical fertilizer. In this respect, Africa more nearly resembles semi-arid Australia, which, despite its technologically advanced farm system, has raised grain yield per hectare only 18 percent over the last 30 years. North America, East Asia, and Western Europe, by contrast, have more than doubled grain yields during that time. (See Table 6.) By comparison with Australia, African agriculture does not fare quite

Table 6: Grain Yield Per Hectare by Region, 1950-52 and 1980-82

Region	Average Yield		Change
	1950-52	1980-82	
	(kilograms)		(percent)
North America	1646	3757	+ 128
Western Europe	1733	3843	+ 122
East Asia	1419	2973	+ 109
Eastern Europe	931	1819	+ 95
South Asia	825	1450	+ 76
South America	1217	1854	+ 52
Africa	757	1044	+ 38
Australia[1]	1100	1301	+ 18
World	1186	2247	+ 89

[1]Data are for 1981-83 to avoid trend distortion.

Source: U.S. Department of Agriculture, Economic Research Service, *World Indices of Agricultural and Food Production, 1950-83* (unpublished printout) (Washington, D.C.: 1984).

as poorly, since grain yield per hectare is up some 38 percent, an increase roughly double that of Australia.

The key to raising cropland productivity in Asia has been irrigation and fertilizer interacting with high-yield dwarf wheats and rices. In Africa, the use of both of these yield-raising inputs has been increasing, though from a small base. Even though irrigated area in Africa has increased from 5.8 million hectares in 1963 to 8.6 million hectares in 1981 (about 7 percent of cropland), it still leaves Africa, a region with 11 percent of the world's people, with only 4 percent of its irrigated area. (See Figure 5.) Within Africa, irrigated area is highly concentrated in a few countries. Egypt, whose agriculture depends on irrigation from the Nile, has 34 percent of Africa's irrigated area. The Sudan, also relying on the Nile, has 21 percent. On the southern end of the continent, South Africa has invested heavily in irrigation,

Million
Hectares

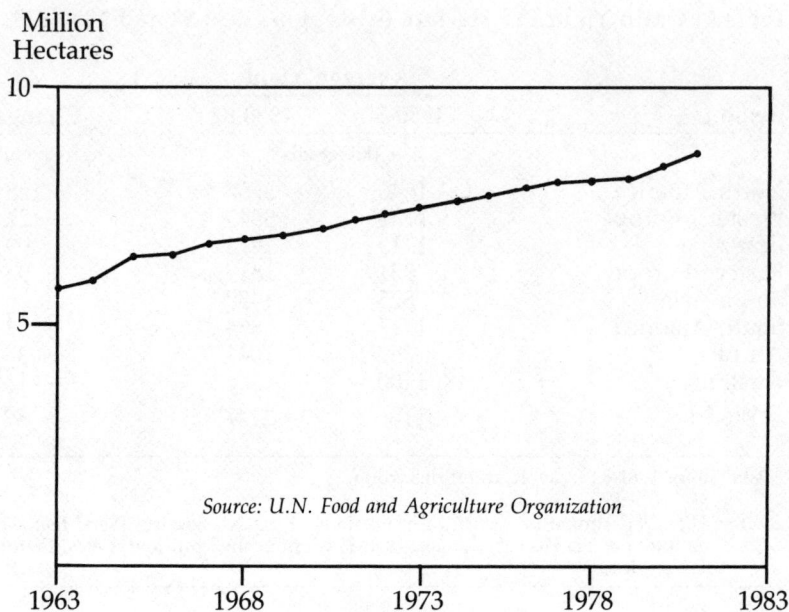

Source: U.N. *Food and Agriculture Organization*

Figure 5: Irrigation in Africa, 1963-81

accounting for 12 percent of the continental total. Together, these three countries have two-thirds of the continent's irrigated land, leaving the remaining one-third to be scattered sparsely throughout the rest of Africa.[97]

Africa's experience with fertilizer has been somewhat similar. Fertilizer use has climbed from negligible levels at mid-century to 3.6 million tons in 1982, but this still amounts to only 3 percent of world fertilizer use. (See Figure 6.) Usage patterns parallel irrigation, with South Africa and Egypt accounting for 55 percent of the continental

Million
Metric
Tons

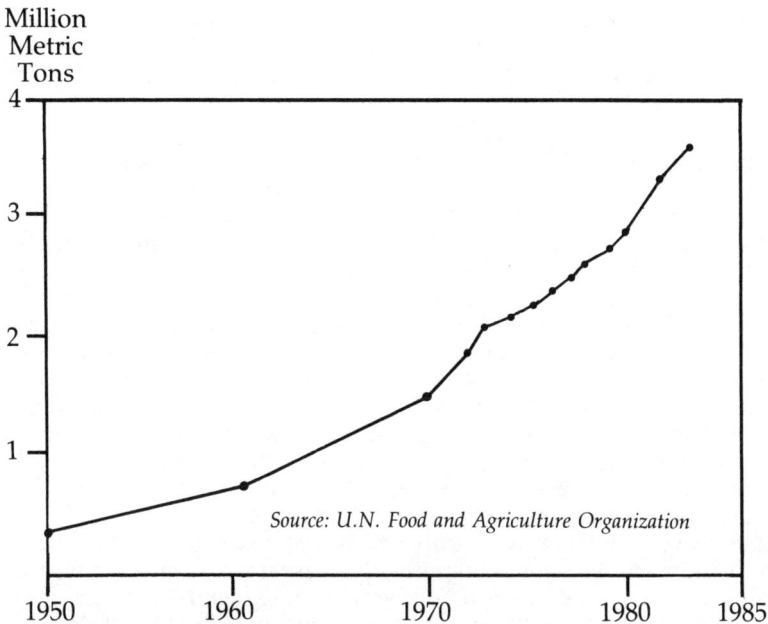

Figure 6: Fertilizer Use in Africa, 1950-82

use.[98] With little fertilizer used outside of Egypt, the Sudan, and South Africa, it comes as no surprise that since 1950 Africa has increased output more from plowing new land than from raising land productivity. This contrasts sharply with the rest of the world, where more than four-fifths of production gains have come from boosting yields.

Although gains in land productivity for Africa as a whole have not been particularly impressive, those in a few countries have been exceptional. South Africa has nearly tripled yields over the last three decades, matching or exceeding the gains in North America, Western Europe, and Japan. Tunisia and Zimbabwe have each more than doubled yields. Egypt, starting from a far higher base, has nearly doubled yields.

On the other end of the spectrum, a number of countries have lower crop yields today than they did a generation ago. Grain yields per hectare in Nigeria, for example, are 3 percent lower today than they were in the early fifties. Yields have declined even more in Mozambique, Zambia, Sudan, and Tanzania. (See Table 7.) In all, more than 40 percent of all Africans live in countries where grain yields per hectare are lower today than they were a generation ago. Yield-raising technologies such as chemical fertilizer and improved varieties have been adopted to at least some extent in all countries. But in some these inputs have been more than offset by soil erosion, the addition of low fertility land to the cropland base, shorter fallow periods, declining rainfall, and inappropriate farm policies. Land productivity has declined most in countries where cultivated area has expanded most, such as Zambia, Nigeria, and the Sudan. (See Figure 7.) In addition to lower inherent fertility, the newly cultivated land typically suffers more from soil erosion, either because it is steeply sloping and vulnerable to water erosion, or because it is semi-arid and more susceptible to wind erosion. Soils on many of Africa's subsistence farms are also suffering from nutrient depletion as firewood shortages lead to the burning of cow dung and crop residues, both traditional fertilizers.

Land productivity has also been influenced by the decline in rainfall over the last two decades. If changes in land use and land degradation are contributing to a long-term decline in rainfall, then efforts to raise Africa's land productivity will face even stiffer odds in the future.

Some segments of African agriculture, such as the irrigated agriculture of Egypt and South Africa, or the rainfed corn production of Zimbabwe, have been developed largely by basic technologies from elsewhere in the world. For most of Africa's agriculture, however, few technologies can be introduced from abroad. Little research has

"More than 40 percent of all Africans
live in countries where grain yields
per hectare are lower today than they
were a generation ago."

Table 7: Grain Yield Per Hectare in Selected African Countries,
1950-52 and 1980-82

Country	Average Yield		Change
	1950-52	1980-82	
	(kilograms)		(percent)
South Africa	758	2,058	+ 171
Tunisia	461	1,005	+ 118
Zimbabwe	649	1,328	+ 104
Egypt	2,248	4,153	+ 85
Ivory Coast	471	791	+ 68
Ethiopia	703	1,066	+ 52
Senegal	439	633	+ 44
Morocco	628	879	+ 40
Uganda	1,127	1,518	+ 35
Kenya	993	1,317	+ 33
Angola	540	584	+ 8
Rwanda	1,122	1,159	+ 3
Ghana	764	774	+ 1
Algeria	648	640	− 1
Nigeria	760	734	− 3
Zaire	902	851	− 6
Mozambique	610	550	− 9
Zambia	952	802	− 16
Sudan	780	636	− 18
Tanzania	1,271	932	− 27

Source: U.S. Department of Agriculture, Economic Research Service, *World Indices of
Agricultural and Food Production, 1950-83*, unpublished printout, (Washington,
D.C.: 1984).

been done, for example, on improving the productivity of trans-
humant pastoralism, a system of livestock husbandry where some or
all of the herding family moves with the herd during part of the year

Kilograms
Per
Hectare

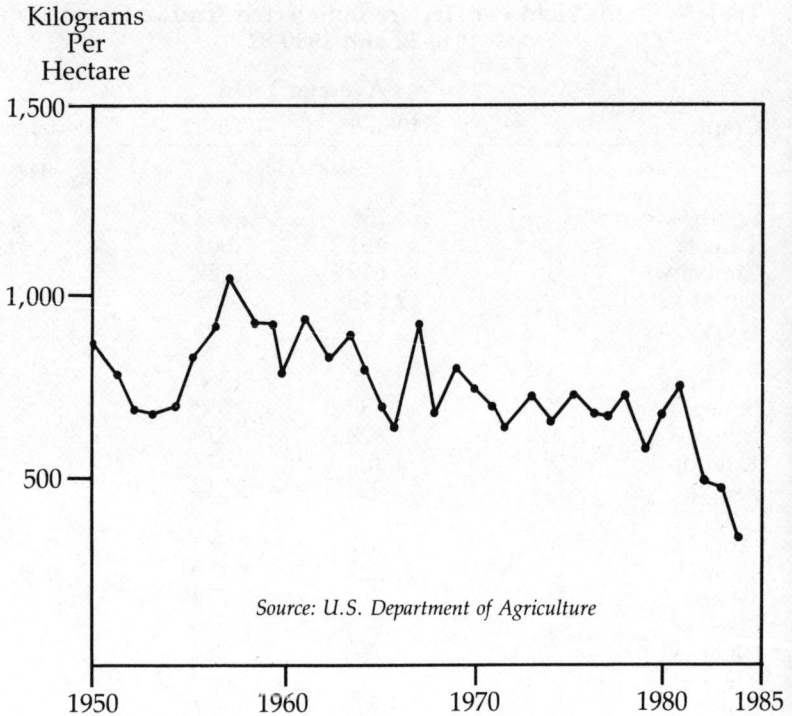

Figure 7: Grain Yield in the Sudan, 1950-84

to take advantage of various seasonal forage sources. In this semi-nomadic livestock production system, technologies or changes in herd management practices that will dramatically boost productivity are difficult to introduce.

Much of African agriculture once consisted of a complex, interactive mixture of crops, livestock, and trees—a system that contrasts sharply with the monocultures on which most of the world's agricultural research is based, and which African farmers have been encouraged to adopt in recent years. What is needed in large areas of Africa, perhaps more than anything else, is a holistic or systems approach to both agricultural research and extension. As World Bank forester Jean Gorse has observed, the people with the information and understanding needed to help design strategies to raise the productivity of farmers and pastoralists in these complex systems are the farmers and pastoralists themselves. This observation suggests that only a more time-consuming approach to project design, one that involves local people in planning, is likely to succeed.[99]

Of all the steps that governments can take to raise agricultural productivity in Africa, a reorientation of food price policies is most important. Too many African governments have followed food price policies designed to placate urban consumers. Ceiling prices discourage agricultural investment and modernization. A better policy would offer government-backed price supports to establish price levels and also provide the assurance that farmers need to invest. In some cases, average prices for farm commodities after the adoption of price supports are little changed from before. But the assurance of minimum prices removes market uncertainty, thus encouraging investment at planting time.

In Zimbabwe, one of the few African countries with effective price supports, both the farmers on large commercial holdings and those on communal lands are responding vigorously to price incentives. With a return to near normal rainfall for the 1985 crop, Zimbabwe will have a large exportable surplus of corn. Farmers on the communal lands alone have produced a record corn surplus estimated at 800,000 tons. Indeed, Zimbabwe announced in April 1985 that it was providing 25,000 tons of grain to Ethiopia as food aid.[100]

Price supports can partly offset other constraints, such as the lack of literacy and of effective agricultural extension systems, as they have, for example, in India over the past two decades. If a technology is obviously profitable, market forces and the demonstration effect will help spread its use from farm to farm.

Until recently, labor was the principal constraint on the productivity of Africa's traditional agricultural production systems. But as the population/land ratio increases, land is becoming the major constraint. Research to identify means of substituting labor for land in the effort to increase productivity could pay high dividends. Among the labor-intensive activities that might effectively boost the land's carrying capacity are tree planting, stall feeding, and composting. When feasible, stall feeding permits a more carefully regulated harvest of forage and the concentration of animal manure in a single location. This in turn facilitates the systematic composting of animal manure with crop residues such as straw, leaves, and other organic materials.

In a continent where livestock figure so prominently as a source of food, draft power, and, increasingly, as a source of fuel, livestock productivity is also an important indicator of overall agricultural productivity. Any successful agricultural strategy will include efforts to increase livestock productivity, either through breeding or better management. In this vein the International Livestock Center for Africa (ILCA), headquartered in Addis Ababa, is crossing European dairy cattle with local draft breeds in an effort to develop a breed of hardy dual-purpose animals that can be used for both plowing and milking. Success would enable farmers to produce food and draft power with fewer animals and less feed.[101]

One long-recognized need of African agriculture is for more drought-resistant millet and sorghum varieties. Closely related is the need for more drought-resistant, faster-growing varieties of multi-purpose trees. The FAO has begun to collect seed and coordinate field trials of useful tree varieties in semi-arid areas; Senegal and Sudan are already cooperating in this effort, and other African countries have been invited to participate.[102]

African governments and the agricultural research community must recognize the need for numerous technological packages for African agriculture. These include technologies that have been developed elsewhere for irrigated agriculture or for dry-land farming, as well as new technologies oriented toward bush fallow cultivation, nomadic pastoralism, agroforestry, and integrated crop-livestock farming.

"The research investment needed to
achieve a given advance in farm
output in Africa may be far greater
than in Asia or North America."

Given the enormous diversity in agricultural systems that characterize the continent, no one package will work for more than a small segment of the continent's farm sector. As a result, the research investment needed to achieve a given advance in farm output in Africa may be far greater than in Asia or in North America.

65

For some segments of African agriculture, no technologies are available to dramatically boost productivity and carrying capacity. In many cases, none are in sight. Agricultural science simply does not yet offer the subsistence farmer in semi-arid conditions as much as it does the market farmer with an abundance of water at his disposal.

Underestimating the extraordinary complexity of the conditions facing agriculture in Africa would be a grave mistake. Africa's agricultural future depends as much on efforts to protect its soils and restore the hydrological balance as on advances in farm technology. But it depends even more on efforts by governments and family planners to quickly slow population growth. Failure on this front virtually ensures failure in the effort to restore an upward trend in per capita food production.

Elements of a Reversal Strategy

The continuation of a "business-as-usual" strategy toward Africa by the international development community is to, in effect, write Africa off. The crisis has prompted a few laudable initiatives, such as World Bank efforts to raise an additional $1 billion for long-term economic assistance to Africa, and the appointment of an Emergency Relief Coordinator for Africa by the United Nations Secretary General. But these actions deal largely with the symptoms of Africa's decline, not the causes. An economic assistance strategy dictated by traditional financial criteria—the rate-of-return on project investments—is destined to fail; indeed, it is already failing.

At issue is whether the imagination and political will exist to arrest the continent-wide ecological deterioration before it leads to further declines in income and a far greater loss of life from starvation. This raises several questions: are the political leaders of Africa prepared to make the tough decisions needed to reverse the decline? And, is the international community prepared to mobilize to help Africa save itself? Can African governments and the international development community adopt a development strategy based on environmental rather than narrow economic goals, one that restores and preserves natural support systems—forests, grasslands, soils, and the hydrological regime—rather than meeting a specified rate of return on investment in a particular project?

An alternative to abandoning rate-of-return criteria is to include all the relevant benefits of a given investment. But for some of the most needed investments, this may exceed existing evaluation skills. For example, the calculation of tree-planting benefits should include not only the value of firewood produced, but also the fertilizer value of cow dung and crop residues that are not burned for fuel, the value of topsoil saved as a result of reduced rainfall runoff, and the beneficial effects of plant transpiration on rainfall recycling—to name a few.

With environmental deterioration undermining economic progress all across Africa, the only successful economic development strategy will be one that restores the natural systems on which the economy depends. Reversing Africa's decline will require carefully orchestrated national efforts to organize millions of people to plant trees, build soil conservation terraces, and plan families. An environmentally oriented effort to reverse trends in Africa will, of necessity, be people-based rather than capital-based. More capital will be needed, much more, but the heart of the reversal strategy will be the mobilization of people.

The effort to avert economic collapse in Africa, similar in spirit to the Marshall Plan that revitalized Western Europe after World War II, will, however, be far more demanding. Africa's population, at over a half billion, is more than double that of Western Europe at the time the Marshall Plan was launched. The Marshall Plan was designed to rebuild war-devastated economies rather than ecologically devastated ones. Europe would have recovered without the Marshall Plan, albeit much more slowly. But Africa is not likely to arrest the ecological deterioration and the economic decline that follows without as-

> "Reversing Africa's decline will
> require carefully orchestrated national
> efforts to organize millions of people
> to plant trees, build soil conservation
> terraces, and plan families."

sistance from abroad. Europe had the basic institutions in place; most of the destruction was physical damage to cities and industrial capacity. Africa does not yet have all the institutions and skills needed to reverse the decline. Europe was geographically compact, with well-developed communication and transport systems. Africa is vast, with only the most rudimentary transporation network. The cost of transporting food from surplus to deficit areas, whether by truck or draft animals, can be prohibitive.

The mobilization of human and capital resources needed to reverse Africia's decline is perhaps more like the emergency mobilization of the Allied Powers in the early forties, which required quick, broad-based action. Had the Allied Powers reacted slowly, the path of events, and even the outcome of World War II, might have been dramatically altered. Faced with an emergency, national governments adopted compulsory military service, imposed rationing, and commandeered industrial facilities and research institutes to achieve wartime goals. Winning the war required a single-mindedness and a unified sense of purpose, including a common appreciation of why sacrifices were needed. A similar effort will be needed to reverse environmental decline in Africa.

Leadership will be needed to coordinate the international effort. In earlier times, the United States provided such leadership. It led the reconstruction of Europe and Japan after World War II. In both 1966 and 1967 it shipped a fifth of its wheat crop to India in a highly successful effort to stave off famine after two monsoon failures in that country. But the United States does not now appear to have the leadership, even if it had the will. Nor are any of the relatively young institutions within Africa yet mature enough to provide this leadership. At the international level, only the World Bank appears to be institutionally strong enough to lead such an effort. But it is not ideally suited for this role. The Bank's experience lies primarily in carrying out large-scale development projects, not in local mobilization of the kind needed in Africa. Despite the need for a philosophical reorientation, the Bank seems destined to fill the leadership role simply because no other international group has the capability.

Success will require an unprecedented degree of cooperation among African countries as well. In April 1980, African heads of state met in Lagos, Nigeria, to endorse the Lagos Plan of Action, a blueprint for the continent's long-term development aimed at economic integration and calling for a strategy of collective self-reliance. Deepening economic crisis has prevented African leaders from making much progress toward these goals. The pervasive environmental deterioration, and its common causes throughout the continent, may provide a focal point for African cooperation that can rekindle the spirit in which the Lagos Plan was conceived.[103]

In the past few years, the UN Economic Commission for Africa, directed by Nigerian Adebayo Adedeji, has taken the lead among African institutions in assessing long-term economic and development trends. The African Development Bank, the continent's key development institution, recently convened a workshop on desertification, signaling its recognition that environmental deterioration diminishes the effectiveness of its lending programs. The Bank's neglect of population issues and policy continues, however. An Institute for Natural Resources in Africa, a body recently proposed by the United Nations University, could marshall the continent's substantial but underused scientific and intellectual resources to help define a resource-based recovery strategy. Several countries, including the Ivory Coast and Zambia, have already expressed interest and offered financial support to found the Institute, and an agreement with the Economic Commission for Africa and the Organization for African Unity is nearly concluded. Such an Institute could strengthen the national institutions needed to underpin successful regional and international initiatives.[104]

As a start, national assessments and long-term projections of environmental, resource, demographic, and economic trends are needed. A similar effort, undertaken in China in the late seventies, provided the foundation for reorienting that country's population, environmental, and agricultural policies. Without a better understanding of where existing trends are leading, it will be difficult to mobilize support to reverse them, either within or outside Africa. Few countries have even attempted to measure topsoil losses from erosion, much less to project the cumulative consequences of continuing losses for land productivity. Assessments are needed of the deterioration of grasslands, the loss of forest cover, changes in the hydrological cycle, soil erosion, and the effect on soil fertility of burning cow dung and crop residues for fuel. Most important, explicit projections of ecological trends will help in analyzing the effect of changes in natural systems on economic trends. Trend projections would also help define the thrust and scale of a successful reversal strategy. Such projections can help national political leaders inform themselves; and they can provide the information to help people understand the need for, and to accept, dramatic new initiatives.

If the economic decline affecting Africa is to be reversed, each country will need an environmentally-based development strategy. The World Bank, given its research capacity and its experience in formulating policies and establishing priorities, is best equipped to assist individual countries in outlining a national development strategy to reverse the broadbased ecological deterioration and set the stage for the resumption of growth in per capita food production and income. If events confirm the possibility that land use changes and soil degradation are altering the hydrological cycle and reducing rainfall, a continental strategy will be needed to reverse the drying-out trend. Given the scale of climatic processes, only a coordinated, continent-wide reversal strategy would have much prospect of success.

Once national strategies are outlined, and goals and timetables established for such things as planting trees and planning families, it would be up to each national government to mobilize its own people and integrate assistance from abroad into the national strategy. Outside assistance can come from international development agencies such as the World Bank, the International Fund for Agricultural Development, and the African Development Bank; the specialized organizations of the United Nations system, such as the UN Fund for Population Activities and the Food and Agriculture Organization; the bilateral aid agencies of the major industrial countries; private development groups, such as CARE and Church World Service; private foundations; and numerous other sources. Without a clearly defined national strategy, neither indigenous resources nor those coming from the outside will be efficiently used.

70

The unprecedented outpouring of private contributions for food aid to Africa by people of the industrial societies suggests support for more extensive government involvement. Young people, in particular, want to help. For young Americans the principal vehicle for this has been the Peace Corps. Bernard Kouchner, the French physician who organized Doctors Without Borders, is urging the countries of the European Community to organize a similiar effort, offering service in the Third World, particularly Africa, as an alternative to military service. From a European point of view, bringing young people—Frenchmen, Danes, Germans, Italians—together for training, would help regain a sense of common European effort and purpose. Kouchner sees these teams, perhaps led by retired people with skills and experience, working at the village level.[105] Opportunities are also plentiful for young professionals and mid-career or retired individuals who can bring particular skills in such fields as agricultural engineering or forestry. One might even envision a World Bank-organized international youth assistance corps, modelled after the Peace Corps, whose staffing and recruitment would be designed to fill the specific skill gaps that emerge as national efforts to reverse recent trends get under way.

Mobilizing people at the local level is more akin to the Peace Corps model than the large-scale, project-oriented approach that has dominated aid to developing countries. This latter approach, most compatible with the industrial world's strengths in administration and management, is a post-colonial development that has proved sadly mismatched to Africa's needs. As one commentator observed: "A way has to be found to reintroduce Western capacity for organization, without old forms of domination, if the cycle of degeneration is to be reversed."[106]

Many of the lessons most relevant to Africa's crisis have been learned not in the developed world but elsewhere in the Third World. South Korean and Chinese successes in national reforestation, Indian and Nepalese experience with village woodlots, and community-based family planning programs in Thailand and Indonesia, where population growth has been halved within a decade, suggest potential partnerships that African leaders might pursue.

"Many of the lessons most relevant to
Africa's crisis have been learned not
in the developed world but elsewhere
in the Third World."

Despite Africa's ecological and cultural diversity, the principal initiatives needed are common to all countries. An all-Africa strategy could perhaps best be visualized in terms of a matrix of countries and the principal actions—family planning, reforestation and soil conservation—that are needed to reverse recent trends. Maintaining current information on each national initiative in a matrix would provide a means of annually evaluating progress to quickly determine where gains were occurring and where deterioration was continuing. This information could then be the basis of an annual progress report that could be issued by the World Bank.

Closely related to such a continent-wide effort would be quick and regular dissemination of information. When rapid change is needed, there is a premium on current information to help guide that change. A monthly periodical that would report African successes, such as those in Zimbabwe's family planning, Kenya's Green Belt movement, or Ethiopia's massive terrace building program, would be invaluable to all national governments.

Africa faces difficult choices. Success in saving Africa hinges on whether political institutions are strong enough to make the course corrections needed to reverse the decline. The ecological handwriting on the wall could not be clearer. The economic consequences of continuing ecological decay are equally clear. The social costs, the human suffering, and loss of life, could eventually approach those of World War II.

Those outside Africa should be concerned with what happens in Africa for several reasons. Reversing Africa's decline represents a test of strength in the effort to arrest environmental deterioration when it threatens the economy. Today Africa is in trouble; tomorrow it could be the Andean countries or the Indian subcontinent.

There are also reasons of self-interest in the industrial countries. If the ecological degradation of Africa continues, so too will pressures that are increasing its external debt, now estimated to reach $170 billion by the end of 1985. Continuing ecological degradation will not only fuel the growth in debt, but it also virtually ensures that African countries will not be able to make future interest payments, much less repay the principal.[107]

72   The greatest risk in Africa is that there will be a loss of hope. However bleak the deteriorating situation may appear, it is of human origin and can yield to human remedy. How African leaders and the international community respond to the challenge will reveal much about the human prospect over the remainder of this century and the beginning of the next one.

Notes

1. U.S. Agency for International Development (AID), "Fiscal Year 1980 Budget Proposal for Ethiopia," Washington, D.C., 1978.

2. Estimate of Africans fed with imported grain in 1984 based on import figures from U.S. Department of Agriculture (USDA), Foreign Agricultural Service, *Foreign Agriculture Circular FG-8-84*, Washington, D.C., May 1984, and on assumption that one ton of grain will feed roughly six people for a year. Assessment of displaced people from United Nations, "Report on the Emergency Situation in Africa," New York, February 22, 1985. Estimate of famine deaths is from UN Economic Commission for Africa (ECA), "Second Special Memorandum by the ECA Conference of Ministers: International Action for Relaunching the Initiative for Long-Term Development and Economic Growth in Africa," Addis Ababa, April 25-29, 1985.

3. USDA, Economic Research Service, *World Indices of Agricultural and Food Production, 1950-84* (unpublished printout)(Washington, D.C.: 1985).

4. ECA, "Second Special Memorandum."

5. ECA, "Report of the Sixth Meeting of the Preparatory Committee of the Whole," Addis Ababa, April 24, 1985; external debt figure from ECA, "Recommendations of the ECA Conference of Ministers of the Twenty-First Ordinary Session of the Assembly of Heads of State and Government of the Organization of African Unity," Addis Ababa, April 25-29, 1985.

6. Kenneth Newcombe, *An Economic Justification for Rural Afforestation: the Case of Ethiopia*, Energy Department Paper No. 16 (Washington, D.C.: The World Bank, 1984).

7. UN Development Program/World Bank Energy Sector Assessment Program, *Ethiopia: Issues and Options in the Energy Sector*, Report No. 4741-ET (Washington, D.C.: World Bank, 1984).

8. Kenneth Newcombe, "Household Energy Supply: The Energy Crisis That Is Here To Stay!" presented to the Senior Policy Seminar—Energy, Sub-Saharan Africa II, Gabarone, Botswana, March 18-22, 1985.

9. United Nations Food and Agriculture Organization (FAO), *Tropical Forest Resources*, Forestry Paper 30 (Rome: 1982); World Bank survey from Gunter Schramm and David J. Jhirad, "Sub-Saharan Africa Policy Paper—Energy" (draft), World Bank, Washington, D.C., August 20, 1984.

10. Schramm and Jhirad, "Sub-Saharan Africa Policy Paper."

11. Livestock population data from FAO, *Production Yearbook* (Rome: various years); human population data from UN Department of International Economic and Social Affairs, *World Population and Its Age-Sex Composition By Country, 1950-2000* (New York: United Nations, 1980); and Population Reference Bureau, *1983 World Population Data Sheet* (Washington, D.C.: 1983).

12. Southern African Development Coordination Conference, *SADCC Agriculture: Toward 2000* (Rome: FAO, 1984).

13. William I. Jones and Roberto Egli, *Farming Systems in Africa*, World Bank Technical Paper Number 27 (Washington, D.C.: World Bank, 1984).

14. Ibid.

15. Dr. Robert S. Kandel, "Mechanisms Governing the Climate of the Sahel: A Survey of Recent Modelling and Observational Studies," Organisation for Economic Co-operation and Development and Permanent Interstate Committee for Drought Control in the Sahel, Paris, October 1984; Jean Gorse, "Desertification in the Sahelian and Sudanian Zones of West Africa," (draft), World Bank, Washington, D.C., February 1985.

16. Reviews of drought in sub-Saharan Africa include Peter J. Lamb, "Persistence of Subsaharan Drought," *Nature*, September 2, 1982; Sharon E. Nicholson, "Sub-Saharan Rainfall in the Years 1976-80: Evidence of Continued Drought," *Monthly Weather Review*, August 1983; Richard A. Kerr, "Fifteen Years of African Drought," *Science*, March 22, 1985; and Stefi Weisburd and Janet Raloff, "Climate and Africa: Why the Land Goes Dry," *Science News*, May 4, 1985.

17. Sharon Nicholson, Florida State University, Tallahassee, Florida, private communication, June 13, 1985.

18. National Research Council, Board on Science and Technology for International Development, *Environmental Change in the West African Sahel* (Washington, D.C.: National Academy Press, 1983).

19. F. Kenneth Hare, "Recent Climatic Experience in the Arid and Semi-Arid Lands," *Desertification Control* (Nairobi), May 1984.

20. Discussed in Kerr, "Fifteen Years of African Drought," and Weisburd and Raloff, "Climate and Africa."

21. J. Shukla and Y. Mintz, "Influence of Land-Surface Evapotranspiration on the Earth's Climate," *Science*, March 19, 1982.

22. Kandel, "Mechanisms Governing the Climate of the Sahel."

23. Moisture recycling discussed in Eneas Salati, Thomas E. Lovejoy, and Peter B. Vose, "Precipitation and Water Recycling in Tropical Rain Forests with Special Reference to the Amazon Basin," *The Environmentalist*, Volume 3, Number 1, 1983; and Eneas Salati and Peter B. Vose, "Amazon Basin: A System in Equilibrium," *Science*, July 13, 1984.

24. F. Kenneth Hare, "Climate and Desertification: A revised analysis," World Meteorological Organization, Geneva, January 1983.

25. Jule Charney, W. J. Quirk, S. Chow, and J. Kornfield, "A Comparative Study of the Effects of Albedo Change on Drought in Semi-Arid Regions," *Journal of the Atmospheric Sciences*, September 1977.

26. Kandel, "Mechanisms Governing the Climate of the Sahel"; Shukla and Mintz, "Influence of Land-Surface Evapotranspiration."

27. Forest data from Shramm and Jhirad, "Sub-Saharan Africa Policy Paper," and FAO, *Tropical Forest Resources*.

28. Area in cereals from USDA, *World Indices*. Total cropland area estimated by Worldwatch Institute based on data from USDA and from World Bank, *Accelerated Development in Sub-Saharan Africa* (Washington, D.C.: 1981).

29. United Nations Sudano-Sahelian Office, *Action Plan--Sahel* (New York: United Nations, 1984).

30. Charles Weiss, "Will the Sahelian Drought Persist?" (draft), World Bank, Washington, D.C., April 1985.

31. FAO, *Tropical Forest Resources*.

32. Salati and Vose, "Amazon Basin."

33. Ibid.

34. F. Kenneth Hare, cited in National Research Council, *Environmental Change*.

35. Population data from UN Department of International Economic and Social Affairs, *World Population and Its Age-Sex Composition*, and Population Reference Bureau, *1985 World Population Data Sheet* (Washington, D.C.: 1985).

36. Hare, "Recent Climatic Experience."

37. Calculated from Population Reference Bureau, *1985 World Population Data Sheet.*

38. UN projections cited in Thomas J. Goliber, "Sub-Saharan Africa: Population Pressures on Development," *Population Bulletin* (Washington, D.C.: Population Reference Bureau, February, 1985).

39. World Bank, *World Development Report 1984* (New York: Oxford University Press, 1984).

40. Ibid. Nigeria's oil prospects discussed in International Energy Agency, *World Energy Outlook* (Paris: Organisation for Economic Co-operation and Development, 1982).

41. Cited in World Bank, *Sub-Saharan Africa: Progress Report on Development Prospects and Programs* (Washington, D.C.: 1983).

42. Goliber, "Sub-Saharan Africa: Population Pressures on Development."

43. Ibid.

44. Cited in Ibid.

45. Roy Stacy, U.S. AID Mission Director, Harare, Zimbabwe, private communication, April 30, 1985.

46. World Fertility Survey data cited in Goliber, "Sub-Saharan Africa: Population Pressures on Development."

47. Population Institute, *Toward Population Stabilization: Findings from Project 1990* (New York: 1984).

48. Rodolfo A. Bulatao, *Expenditures on Population Programs in Developing Regions: Current Levels and Future Requirements*, Staff Working Paper No. 679 (Washington, D.C.: World Bank, 1985); World Bank, *World Development Report 1984.*

49. Anders Wijkman and Lloyd Timberlake, *Natural Disasters: Acts of God or acts of Man?* (London and Washington, D.C.: Earthscan, 1984).

50. Cropland expansion since 1920 from J.F. Richards, Jerry S. Olson, and Ralph M. Rotty, *Development of a Data Base for Carbon Dioxide Releases Resulting From Conversion of Land to Agricultural Uses* (Oak Ridge, Tenn.: Institute for

Energy Analysis, 1983). Comparison of cropland expansion rates in Africa and Asia from John W. Mellor, "The Changing World Food Situation," *Food Policy Statement*, International Food Policy Research Institute, Washington, D.C., January 1985.

51. African river sediment loads discussed in Michael Stocking, "Rates of erosion and sediment yield in the African environment," in D. E. Walling, S. S. D. Foster, and P. Wurzel, eds., *Challenges in African Hydrology and Water Resources* (Oxfordshire, England: International Association of Hydrological Sciences, 1984). Wollo province example from Soil Conservation Research Project, *Compilation of Phase 1 Progress Reports* (Addis Ababa: June 1984).

52. Hans E. Jahnke and Getachew Asamenew, *An Assessment of the Recent Past and Present Livestock Situation in the Ethiopian Highlands* (Addis Ababa: Government of Ethiopia and FAO, 1984).

53. Rwanda example in Jones and Egli, *Farming Systems*.

54. Jan Raath, "Zimbabwe peasants reap huge harvest," *Christian Science Monitor*, April 17, 1985.

55. World Bank, *Accelerated Development in Sub-Saharan Africa*.

56. Jones and Egli, *Farming Systems*.

57. Hans Hurni, Soil Conservation Research Project, Addis Ababa, private communications, January 9 and February 13, 1985.

58. Soil Conservation Research Project, *Compilation of Phase I Progress Reports*.

59. Swedish International Development Authority, *Soil Conservation in Kenya 1980 Review* (Stockholm: December 1980); "Soil Conservation in Kenya: An Interview with Carl-Gosta Wenner," *Ambio*, Vol. 12, No. 6, 1983.

60. Ibid.

61. Jones and Egli, *Farming Systems*.

62. Stocking, "Rates of Erosion."

63. R. Lal, *No-Till Farming*, Monograph No. 2 (Ibadan, Nigeria: International Institute of Tropical Agriculture, 1983).

64. International Institute of Tropical Agriculture (IITA), *Tasks for the Eighties: An appraisal of progress* (Ibadan, Nigeria: April 1983).

65. Jones and Egli, *Farming Systems*.

66. M.J. Swift, ed., "Soil Biological Processes and Tropical Soil Fertility: A Proposal for a Collaborative Programme of Research," *Biology International*, Special Issue—5, 1984.

67. Quoted in "Center Highlights," *News from CGIAR* (Washington, D.C.), Volume 4, Number 4, December 1984.

68. Jones and Egli, *Farming Systems*. For a thorough introduction to agroforestry, see National Research Council, Board on Science and Technology for International Development, *Agroforestry in the West African Sahel* (Washington, D.C.: National Academy Press, 1984).

69. IITA, *Annual Report 1983* (Ibadan: 1984).

70. Peter Felker, Texas A&I University, Kingsville, Texas, cited in National Research Council, *Agroforestry*.

71. FAO, *Tropical Forest Resources*.

72. Dennis Anderson and Robert Fishwick, *Fuelwood Consumption and Deforestation in African Countries*, Staff Working Paper No. 704 (Washington, D.C.: World Bank, 1984).

73. Anne de Lattre and Arthur M. Fell, *The Club du Sahel: An Experiment in International Cooperation* (Paris: Organisation for Economic Co-operation and Development, 1984); Club du Sahel, "Food Self-Sufficiency and Ecological Balance in the Sahel Countries," Paris, May 27, 1982.

74. U.S. AID, Bureau for Africa, *Energy, Forestry and Natural Resources Activities in the Africa Region* (Washington, D.C: January 1984); John Spears, "Review of World Bank Financed Forestry Activity FY1984," Washington, D.C., June 30, 1984.

75. Spears, "Review of World Bank Financed Forestry Activity."

76. FAO data cited in Office of Technology Assessment, *Technologies to Sustain Tropical Forest Resources* (Washington, D.C.: U.S. Government Printing Office, 1984).

77. Plantation share of fuelwood supply from Anderson and Fishwick, *Fuelwood Consumption and Deforestation.* For economic analysis of reforestation programs, see Newcombe, *An Economic Justification for Rural Afforestation*, and UN Development Program/World Bank Energy Sector Assessment Program, *Ethiopia: Issues and Options.*

78. UN Development Program/World Bank Energy Sector Assessment Program, *Ethiopia: Issues and Options.*

79. T.M. Catterson, "AID Experience in the Forestry Sector in the Sahel— Opportunities for the Future," presented to the Meeting of the Steering Committee, CILSS/Club du Sahel, Paris, June 14-15, 1984.

80. Newcombe, *An Economic Justification for Rural Afforestation.*

81. Anderson and Fishwick, *Fuelwood Consumption and Deforestation.*

82. J.B. Raintree and B. Lundgren, "Agroforestry Potentials for Biomass Production in Integrated Land Use Systems," presented at Biomass Energy Systems: Building Blocks for Sustainable Development, a conference sponsored by the World Resources Institute and the Rockefeller Brothers Fund, Airlie, Virginia, January 29-February 1, 1985.

83. Catterson, "AID Experience in the Forestry Sector."

84. Erik Eckholm, Gerald Foley, Geoffrey Barnard, and Lloyd Timberlake, *Fuelwood: The Energy Crisis That Won't Go Away* (London and Washington, D.C.: Earthscan, 1984).

85. Ibid.

86. UN Development Program/World Bank Energy Sector Assessment Program, *Ethiopia: Issues and Options in the Energy Sector.*

87. Fred R. Weber, "Technical Update on Forestry Efforts in Africa," in AID, Bureau for Africa, *Report of Workshop on Forestry Program Evaluation* (Washington, D.C.: August 1984).

88. Edward S. Ayensu, "Natural and Applied Sciences and National Advancement," presented to the Ghana Academy of Arts and Sciences, Accra, Ghana, November 22, 1984.

89. Dr. Y. Dommergues, "Using Biotechnologies for Improving the Forest

Cover of the Sahelian and Sudanian Zones," presented to the World Bank, Washington, D.C., April 17, 1984; National Research Council, *Environmental Change*.

80

90. Michael Dow, National Research Council, private communication, March 27, 1985.

91. Anderson and Fishwick, *Fuelwood Consumption and Deforestation*.

92. Constance Holden, "Is Bioenergy Stalled?" *Science*, March 1, 1985; "Expanding the Greenbelt," *Connexions* 15, Winter 1985; Jeffrey Gritzner, National Research Council, private communication, March 7, 1985.

93. Weber, "Technical Update."

94. Ernest Stern, Senior Vice President, Operations, "The Evolving Role of the Bank in the 1980s," presented to the Agriculture Symposium, World Bank, Washington, D.C., January 13, 1984.

95. IITA, *Tasks for the Eighties: A Long-range Plan* (Ibadan, Nigeria: June 1981).

96. Ibid.

97. FAO, *Production Yearbook*.

98. FAO, *Fertilizer Yearbook* (Rome: various years).

99. Gorse, "Desertification in the Sahelian and Sudanian Zones."

100. Robbie Mupawose, Secretary of Agriculture, Harare, Zimbabwe, private communication, April 30, 1985.

101. Peter Brumby, International Livestock Center for Africa (ILCA), Addis Ababa, private communication, April 29, 1985; see also ILCA, *Annual Report 1983* (Addis Ababa: 1984).

102. Christel Palmberg, FAO, Rome, private communication, May 17, 1985.

103. For a thorough discussion of the Lagos Plan, see Robert S. Browne and Robert J. Cummings, *The Lagos Plan of Action vs. the Berg Report* (Washington D.C.: African Studies and Research Program, Howard University, 1984).

104. See, for example, ECA, *ECA and Africa's Development 1983-2008* (Addis Ababa: April 1983); African Development Bank (Abidjan), "Desertification and Economic and Social Development in Africa," summary remarks at the 1985 Annual Meeting Symposium, Brazzaville, Congo, May 8, 1985; and United Nations University, *Institute for Natural Resources in Africa: Prospectus* (Tokyo: April 15, 1985).

105. David K. Willis, "European youth eager to help in third world," *Christian Science Monitor*, April 18, 1985; Flora Lewis, "A Risk for Africa," *New York Times*, March 18, 1985.

106. Lewis, "A Risk for Africa."

107. External debt from ECA, "Recommendations of the ECA Conference of Ministers."

LESTER R. BROWN is President and Senior Researcher with Worldwatch Institute and Project Director of the Institute's annual *State of the World* reports. Formerly Administrator of the International Agricultural Development Service of the U.S. Department of Agriculture, he is author of several books including *World Without Borders, By Bread Alone, The Twenty-Ninth Day,* and *Building a Sustainable Society.*

EDWARD C. WOLF is a Senior Researcher with Worldwatch Institute and a coauthor of *State of the World 1985.* He is a graduate of Williams College with a degree in Biology and Environmental Studies.

THE WORLDWATCH PAPER SERIES

No. of
Copies

_____ **Total Copies**

Single Copy—$4.00

Bulk Copies (any combination of titles)
2-5: $3.00 each   5-20: $2.00 each   21 or more: $1.00 each

Calendar Year Subscription (1985 subscription begins with Paper 63)
U.S. $25.00 _____

Make check payable to Worldwatch Institute
1776 Massachusetts Avenue NW, Washington, D.C. 20036 USA

Enclosed is my check for U.S. $ _____

_____
name

_____
address

_____
city   **state**   **zip/country**